THE WILSON ADMINISTRATION
AND
CIVIL LIBERTIES

THE WILSON ADMINISTRATION AND CIVIL LIBERTIES

•

1917-1921

by

HARRY N. SCHEIBER

QUID PRO BOOKS
New Orleans, Louisiana

THE WILSON ADMINISTRATION AND CIVIL LIBERTIES, 1917-1921

Copyright © 1960, 2013 by Harry N. Scheiber. No part of this book may be reproduced by any mechanical, photographic, or electronic process, or other recording, nor may it be stored in a retrieval system, transmitted, or otherwise copied for public or private use—other than for "fair use"—without the written permission of the author or the current publisher. Author photograph courtesy of UC Berkeley Law School.

Originally published in 1960 by Cornell University Press, Ithaca, New York, as Volume VI of the series *Cornell Studies in American History, Literature, and Folklore*.

Published in 2013 by Quid Pro Books, in the series *Legal History & Biography*.

ISBN 978-1-61027-176-9 (pbk.)
ISBN 978-1-61027-175-2 (eBook)

QUID PRO BOOKS
Quid Pro, LLC
5860 Citrus Blvd., suite D-101
New Orleans, Louisiana 70123
www.quidprobooks.com

For Jane

Preface

The years of Woodrow Wilson's second Presidential administration comprise a crucial chapter in the story of civil liberties in the United States. On the eve of American entry into World War I, Wilson expressed the fear that a "spirit of ruthless brutality" would infect "the Congress, the courts, the policeman on the beat, the man in the street."[1] His apprehensions proved fully justified. That spirit also infected some of the members of Wilson's Cabinet, much of the federal bureaucracy, and—to a certain extent—the President himself. In the pages that follow, I attempt to analyze the federal legislation which abridged traditional American liberties, the actual administration of the statutes, and the manner in which federal officials contributed to the climate of opinion in these tumultuous years of war.

This book is a revision of a thesis written in the History Department of Cornell University. My research was conducted under supervision of Professor Dexter Perkins, and I gratefully acknowledge my indebtedness to him. I have benefited from the generosity of many other scholars and archivists, but can mention only Dean Emeritus Harry J. Carman and Professor Richard Hofstadter of Columbia University, whose interest in the work of a former student is only one facet of their kindness; the staffs of the Regional History Collection, Cornell University, and the Manuscripts Division, Library of Congress; and Professors Curtis P. Nettels, Robert H. Elias, and

---

[1] Quoted in John L. Heaton, comp., *Cobb of "The World"* (New York, 1924), 206.

Andrew Hacker of the committee which awarded this study Cornell's Moses Coit Tyler Prize for 1959.

Finally, I wish to extend my thanks to Mrs. Woodrow Wilson for permission to quote from the manuscript and published papers of former President Wilson; Messrs. T. W. Gregory, Jr., and Herman Kahn for permission to quote from unpublished letters of former Attorney General Thomas W. Gregory and Franklin D. Roosevelt, respectively; Doubleday & Company, Inc., for permission to quote from Ray Stannard Baker, *Woodrow Wilson: Life and Letters* (copyright 1931, 1937, 1939, by Ray Stannard Baker); and the Pennsylvania Historical Association, for permission to incorporate materials used in my note, "The Political Career of A. Mitchell Palmer: A Comment," *Pennsylvania History*, XXVI (October, 1959).

H. N. S.
1960

Contents

Page numbers below to the left reference the pagination of the original 1960 print edition. These numbers are inserted into the present text by the use of {brackets}. The pagination of this reprint edition is shown below to the right, and appears at the top of most pages. The original pagination is retained and embedded for the convenience of readers and researchers, for functionality with the new parallel eBook editions, and to allow the Index to have continuity.

Preface ... vi i
I.   The Prewar Years ... 1 1
II.   Security Measures ... 11 13
III.   Censorship ... 29 35
IV.   The Justice Department ... 42 51
V.   The Red Scare ... 52 63
Conclusion ... 59 71
Appendix: Criminal Prosecutions under
the Espionage Act ... 61 73
Bibliographical Note ... 65 79
Index ... 67 81
About the Author 89

First class stamp, 1998, commemorating
Woodrow Wilson and the war effort

THE WILSON ADMINISTRATION
AND
CIVIL LIBERTIES

I • The Prewar Years

IN A JULY Fourth address in 1913, President Wilson expressed with characteristically bold confidence his faith in the unity of the nation. This speech reflected the vision and determination with which he had presented his program of the "New Freedom" that year. "Here is a great people," he said, "great with every force that has ever beaten in the lifeblood of mankind. And it is secure. There is no one within its borders, there is no power among the nations of the earth, to make it afraid...."[1] Wilson promised that day that the battle for social justice had only begun.

When war broke out in Europe a little more than a year later, Americans were shocked and frightened. The President immediately expressed the hope that the United States might remain a nation "that neither sits in judgment upon others nor is disturbed in her own counsels." He urged the people to subordinate their prejudices to a higher purpose. "It will be easy to excite passion and difficult to allay it," he warned. Passion would only bring involvement in the war, "in impulse and opinion if not in action."[2]

For more than a year this was the common theme in Wilson's public pronouncements; the United States, he argued, must stand ready to offer its services as a mediator. Therefore, the American people {2} must remain neutral "in fact as well as in name ... and impartial in

---

[1] R. S. Baker and W. E. Dodd, eds., *The Public Papers of Woodrow Wilson* (New York, 1925–1927), III, 42. Hereinafter cited as *Public Papers*.

[2] Proclamation of Aug. 19, 1914, *ibid.*, 158.

thought as well as in action."[3] Partisanship would render the United States incapable of mediating.

Most Americans in 1914 believed as did the President that the European war was a clash of militarisms whose outcome would not affect the vital interests of the United States. There certainly was no popular desire for intervention. Hence the proclamation of neutrality issued by the government and Wilson's appeal for "neutrality in thought" were welcomed by the nation.[4]

The Preparedness Campaign

Believing that American participation would be confined to mediation, President Wilson opposed—until July, 1915—any increase in United States military power. He feared that a rush to arms would dignify the nationalistic and militaristic elements who favored intervention.[5] The early advocates of preparedness were generally anti-Wilson, pro-British, and highly nationalistic: men such as Theodore Roosevelt, or Augustus Gardner, who "had been sedulously promoting American power for the past two decades."[6] Willard Straight, who was prominent in the preparedness movement in New York, wrote in early

---

[3] *Ibid.*; Address at New York, April 20,1915, *ibid.*, 302–303.

[4] Arthur S. Link, *Woodrow Wilson and the Progressive Era, 1910–1917* (New York, 1954), 148.

[5] Robert E. Osgood, *Ideals and Self-Interest in America's Foreign Relations* (Chicago, 1953), 200–205; Arthur A. Ekirch, Jr., *The Civilian and the Military* (New York, 1956), 154–162.

[6] Osgood, *Ideals and Self-Interest*, 204. See also John Blum, "Nativism, Anti-Radicalism, and the Foreign Scare, 1917–1920," *Midwest Journal*, III (1950–1951), 48; Merle Curti, The Roots of American Loyalty (New York, 1946), 224–225. The Administration worked closely with the liberal opponents of preparedness when Representative Gardner sought an investigation of the military establishment at the end of 1914 (Oswald G. Villard to Joseph Tumulty, Dec. 11, 1914, Woodrow Wilson Papers, Library of Congress; hereinafter cited as Wilson Papers).

1915 that he despised the German people and that it behooved an American to be pro-British.⁷ {3} Straight handled Franco-British copper purchases in the United States for J. P. Morgan and Company; he soon grew impatient with Wilson, whose policy Straight termed that of a jellyfish.⁸ Until the *Lusitania* incident in May, 1915, men such as Straight found their influence confined largely to the Northeast. They were out of tune with both the antimilitarist tradition of American democracy and the public's aloof attitude toward the war.⁹

The sinking of the *Lusitania* marked a turning point in the history of the preparedness campaign and in the history of American neutrality. This disaster forced many citizens to realize that American involvement in the war was a definite if not immediate possibility. As a result, the controversial features of Wilson's position on neutral rights became more significant, and a full-scale national debate ensued. While this debate raged, preparedness ceased to be exclusively the aim of a hopeless minority.¹⁰

Finally, the President reversed his position on rearmament. On July 21, 1915 (the same day that he dispatched the third *Lusitania* note, a stern warning to Germany), Wilson ordered his Cabinet to draft plans for

---

⁷ Letter to Herbert [Croly], March 1, 1915, Willard Straight Papers, Regional History Library, Cornell University. For material relating to Straight's role in the New York City Mayor's Committee for National Defense, see Box 5, *ibid.*

⁸ Letter to Theodore Roosevelt, March 25, 1916, *ibid.;* typescript diary of Willard Straight, January–February, 1915, *ibid.* Straight favored a firm alliance of American with British and French economic interests (Straight to Colonel House, March 17, 1916, *ibid.*).

⁹ Link, *Progressive Era,* 177.

¹⁰ *Ibid.,* 178–179; Osgood, *Ideals and Self-Interest,* 205–206.

rearmament, so that he might present a program to Congress in December.[11]

The Opponents of Preparedness

Many groups in American society which had supported the President's opposition to rearmament prior to the *Lusitania* incident now parted ways with Wilson, for they believed that America was drifting into war with Germany and that preparedness would merely hasten the process. An American militaristic movement underwritten by the munitions makers and supernationalists was the real threat to American neutrality: so believed many liberals and progressives such as Amos Pinchot, Oswald Garrison Villard, {4} Robert La Follette, and George Norris. The progressives who opposed preparedness were supported by significant numbers among Irish-Americans and German-Americans. Socialists and other radical groups regarded the war as a capitalists' fight, and, with the doctrinaire pacifists, also opposed intervention. Finally, there were many Americans who simply did not believe that the national interest required abandoning traditional isolationist policies for the sake of involvement in a European war.[12]

---

[11] R. S. Baker, *Woodrow Wilson: Life and Letters* (New York, 1927–1939), VI, 8–9. Quotations from this work are reprinted by permission of Doubleday and Co., Inc.

[12] In September, 1915, Assistant Secretary of the Navy Franklin Roosevelt wrote of a "paid propaganda organized by the extremists, which is hurting the efforts of those who are soberly and rationally considering National Defense" (letter to Wilson, Sept. 3, 1915, Wilson Papers). Wilson too was suspicious of the preparedness faction and regretted his break with liberals and progressives who opposed rearmament (Wilson to Villard, Nov. 2, 1915, *ibid.;* Wilson to Jane Addams, Nov. 2, 1915, *ibid.;* see also Merle Curti, *Peace or War: The American Struggle* [New York, 1936], 234, 247; Oscar Handlin, *The American People in the 20th Century* [Cambridge, 1954], 116–122; Oswald G. Villard, *Fighting Years* [New York, 1939], 309; H. C. Peterson and G. C. Fite, *Opponents of War, 1917–1918* [Madison, 1957], (*passim*). Rabbi Stephen S. Wise warned

By July 1915 President Wilson was convinced that the United States might need to intervene in Europe, and from that date forward Wilson became increasingly more intolerant of the opponents of rearmament.

Wilson had often asserted his belief in the broad value of the foreign-born in enriching American life. He had insisted, furthermore, that America enjoyed special qualifications to mediate in Europe because of its heterogeneity.[13] Prior to the *Lusitania* crisis Wilson deplored equally the activities of the pro-British preparedness advocates and of the pro-German propagandists.[14] As late as October, 1915, only one month before his armaments program was {5} made public, the President told the Daughters of the American Revolution, assembled in Washington, that "America stands apart in its ideals; it ought not to allow itself to be drawn, so far as its heart is concerned, into anybody's quarrel.... America has a great cause which is not confined to the American continent. It is the cause of humanity itself."[15]

It is significant that in his speech before the D.A.R. Wilson singled out aliens and naturalized citizens as objects of widely held suspicion. He himself believed that most foreign-born Americans were loyal, he asserted. "But I am in a hurry," he added, "for an opportunity to have a line-up and let the men who are thinking first of other countries stand on one side and all those that are

---

Wilson that the most ardent preparedness groups would not be satisfied with anything short of full-scale rearmament (letter to Wilson, Nov. 14, 1915, Wilson Papers). Charles W. Eliot was among the liberals who, like Wilson, apparently distrusted some of the foremost advocates of preparedness, yet believed rearmament to be necessary (see Eliot to George T. Reyes, Oct. 13, 1915, National Civil Service Reform League Papers, Regional History Collection, Cornell University Library).

[13] Address of April 20, 1915, *Public Papers,* III, 304.

[14] *Ibid.,* 307.

[15] Address of Oct. 11, 1915, *ibid.,* 378.

for America first, last, and all the time on the other side."[16] Wilson was fully aware that many of the foreign-born opposed what they considered his pro-British foreign policy, and they would certainly oppose his revised position on preparedness. When, two months later, Wilson presented his armaments program to Congress, he spoke in significantly harsher terms about the foreign-born opponents of his policy. Indeed, he accused them of having "poured the poison of disloyalty into the very arteries of our national life."[17]

The Third Annual Message to Congress

Congress assembled to hear President Wilson's third Annual Message on December 7, 1915. The two major features of the message concerned the rearmament program and the need for legislation to suppress disloyal activity.[18] Many of the arguments presented in this speech were to become major themes in the 1916 Presidential campaign, and the harsh rhetoric was of importance to the debate on American neutrality.

Wilson asserted that the war had extended in scope so as to affect {6} even the Western Hemisphere. He defined the conditions under which the United States would resort to armed defense and demanded increased appropriations for the support of enlarged military and naval establishments.[19]

---

[16] *Ibid.*, 379.

[17] This and all the following quotations from Wilson's Message of Dec. 7, 1915, are taken from the *Congress. Rec.*, LIII (64th Cong., 1st Sess.), 95–100.

[18] The section of the speech relating to inter-American understanding is discussed in Dexter Perkins, *A History of the Monroe Doctrine* (Boston, 1955), 322–324, and Arthur P. Whitaker, *The Western Hemisphere Idea* (Ithaca, 1954), 123–125.

[19] For a discussion of the armaments program, which satisfied neither the preparedness extremists nor the opponents of prepar-

In spite of an uneasy truce with Germany on the issue of neutral rights, Wilson asserted that, in warning against aggression, he had "no thought of any immediate or particular danger arising out of our relations with other nations." What, then, was in fact the menace to American security? The President's explanation was that "the gravest threats against our national peace and safety have been uttered within our own borders. There are citizens of the United States, I blush to admit, born under other flags but welcomed by our generous naturalization laws to the full freedom and opportunity of America, who have poured the poison of disloyalty into the very arteries of our national life."

Wilson accused them of sabotage, sedition, and "conspiracies against the neutrality of the Government." He urged Congress to provide legislation with which their activities might be curbed. Such laws, he stated, were the means by which "such creatures of passion, disloyalty, and anarchy" might be "crushed out."

"The Gravest Threats"

President Wilson launched this broad attack upon the "disloyal" at the insistence of Joe Tumulty, his secretary and closest political adviser. In November, while Wilson was drafting his message, Tumulty sent to Wilson a memorandum urging him to include a request for legislation to curb sabotage and subversion. Wilson had rejected this idea once before. Tumulty insisted, however, that the country was "dissatisfied with our seeming indifference toward the propaganda initiated by our hyphenated friends." The message, he wrote, should in-

---

edness, see Baker, *Life and Letters,* VI, 18; and Link, *Progressive Era,* 182 ff.

clude a strongly worded attack upon those who would "poison and control public opinion."[20]

German propaganda and espionage were undoubtedly disturbing {7} to Wilson, yet he was initially reluctant to include these subjects in his message to Congress. This reluctance was probably born of his determination to assert that America was at peace with every foreign nation, and thereby to reassure antimilitarist opponents of his preparedness plan. Any reference to the recently disclosed hostile activities of German and Austrian officials in the United States would constitute an admission that relations with Germany had reached a dangerous pass.[21] Furthermore, Colonel House was en route to Europe to initiate peace discussions. Thus Wilson accepted Tumulty's advice, but he decided to phrase his message to Congress so as to draw public attention away from the German government, and focus it upon disloyal foreign-born Americans. An appeal to patriotism is always politically safe in a time of stress.

Wilson thus abandoned his position, stated before the D.A.R. in October, that the number of disloyal foreign-born was insignificant. He denounced the foreign-born as responsible for "the gravest threats against our national peace and safety." Unfortunately Wilson cast a shadow of suspicion upon the loyalty of all the foreign-born at a time when he might better have attested to the

---

[20] Quoted in John Blum, *Joe Tumulty and the Wilson Era* (Boston, 1951), 102.

[21] The workings of the $25,000,000 German propaganda effort were made public in August, 1915; a few days before Wilson addressed Congress, the German military and naval embassy attachés were declared *persona non grata* because of their role in sabotaging American munitions plants and ships (J. L. O'Brian, "New Encroachments on Individual Freedom," *Harvard Law Review*, LXVI [1952], 5–6; Carl Wittke, *German-Americans and the World War* [Columbus, 1936], 24; Link, *Progressive Era*, 147, 167).

loyalty of most of them. The leadership of the preparedness movement—drawn for the most part from conservative business groups—had "reidentified hyphenism and radicalism" in the public consciousness.[22] The opponents of preparedness were drawn in large part from the ranks of Irish- and German-Americans, Socialists, pacifists, and progressives, and they had been treated "as one common enemy" by many of the advocates of rearmament;[23] e.g., Straight's condemnation of the La Follette Seamen's Act as the work of a German steamship lobby[24] automatically introduced {8} the question of fundamental loyalties. Borrowing from the rhetoric of preparedness, Wilson repeatedly questioned the patriotism of his political opponents, thus contributing significantly to the worst corollary of the movement—the atmosphere of suspicion and intolerance in which conformity was made a test of loyalty and in which nativism and repression flourished.

Absent from Wilson's speeches in 1916 were his former expressions of faith in the value of heterogeneity. Of the melting pot, the President now asked, "What kind of fire of pure passion are you going to keep burning under the pot in order that the mixture that comes out may be purged of its dross and may be the fine gold of untainted Americanism?"[25]

Americanism, 1916

The members of Congress received the President's December message with mixed reactions. Only once, the New York *Times* reported, did Wilson evoke "unre-

---

[22] Blum, *Midwest Journal,* III, 48. Baker suggests that Wilson feared foreign influences "possibly too strongly" (*Life and Letters,* VI, 256).

[23] Blum, *Midwest Journal*, III, 48.

[24] Letter to Herbert [Croly], March 1, 1915, Straight Papers.

[25] Address of May 20, 1916, Public Papers, IV, 180.

strained enthusiasm." This was, of course, in response to his statements condemning disloyalty.[26] The editorial writers of virtually every major American newspaper commended Wilson's attack on disloyalty, whatever their differences of opinion regarding other portions of the message.[27] The German-American press was, however, almost unanimous in objecting to the President's demand for "a law against German-Americans."[28] Wilson's patriotic appeal had proved itself capable of successful political exploitation, and 1916 was an election year.

When Democratic party leaders planned their campaign prior to the June convention, Wilson insisted that "Americanism" be a major theme. He was active in drafting the party platform and exhibited especial interest in the plank on loyalty,[29] which condemned "every group ... that has for its object the advancement of the interest of a foreign power ... or [whose object] is calculated {9} and tends to divide our people into antagonistic groups and thus to destroy that complete agreement and solidarity of the people ... so essential to the perpetuity of free institutions."[30]

On the eve of the convention Wilson spoke before a Flag Day gathering in Washington and offered a hint of what was to be his personal campaign appeal. Insisting that disloyalty was active in the United States, proceeding from "a very active and subtle minority," he deplored any compromise with "political blackmail."[31]

---

[26] New York *Times*, Dec. 8, 1915.

[27] *Ibid.*

[28] Cincinnati *Volksblatt,* Dec. 9, 1915, quoted in Wittke, *German-Americans,* 43.

[29] Baker, *Life and Letters,* VI, 256.

[30] Democratic National Committee, *Democratic Text-Book,* 1916 (New York, 1916).

[31] *Public Papers,* IV, 209.

Throughout the convention and the campaign Democratic politicians reiterated the assertion that "he kept us out of war." Wilson, however, gave equal emphasis to the issue of Americanism in his own speeches.[32] Formally opening his campaign in September, Wilson attacked "certain active groups and combinations of men amongst us who were born under foreign flags." These men, he declared, had "injected the poison of disloyalty into our own most critical affairs, laid violent hands upon many of our industries, and subjected us to the shame of divisions of sentiment and purpose in which America was contemned and forgotten." As for tolerance, Wilson had said that Americans should "teach these gentlemen once for all that loyalty to this flag is the first test of tolerance."[33] In one of the most widely publicized incidents of the campaign, Wilson replied in September to Jeremiah O'Leary, inflexibly anti-British Irish-American leader who had requested definition of Wilson's views concerning the war: "I would feel deeply mortified to have you or anybody else like you vote for me. Since you have access to many disloyal Americans and I have not, I will ask you to convey this message to them."[34] It was then revealed that the Republican nominee, Charles Evans Hughes, had secretly obtained O'Leary's {10} approval of his projected foreign policy, and Hughes was forced to make a statement of repudiation on October 25.[35]

It is difficult to assess the effects of Wilson's "Americanism" campaign upon the outcome of the election. Both Republican and Democratic politicians sought to attract the "hyphenate" vote, if such was in fact significantly

---

[32] *Ibid., passim.*

[33] *Ibid.,* 283, 209. For a suggestive commentary by a racist on the issue of the hyphenate American, see Thomas Dixon to Wilson, Sept. 30, 1916, in File VI, 2247, Wilson Papers.

[34] Baker, *Life and Letters,* VI, 290.

[35] *Ibid.*

coherent. Furthermore, Theodore Roosevelt's bellicose campaign on behalf of Hughes offered adequate solace to the Republican nativist or interventionist who might be displeased with Hughes's timidity. Perhaps it is true, as contemporary analysts concluded, that "the key factor in Democratic success was Wilson's and his party's promise of continued peace, prosperity, and progressive democracy."[36]

Yet the fact remains that Wilson questioned the loyalty of the foreign-born in the United States. By so presenting the issues, the President contributed to the ferment of intolerance in which superpatriotism was to flourish during the tense years of war to come.

---

[36] Link, *Progressive Era*, 250. See also Dexter Perkins, *Charles Evans Hughes and American Democratic Statesmanship* (Boston, 1956), 55, 60–61, in which Hughes's campaign is criticized; Carl Wittke, *The German-Language Press in America* (Lexington, 1957), 255 ff; C. J. Child, *The German-American in Politics, 1914–1917* (Madison, 1939).

II • Security Measures

DESPITE the ostensibly cordial reception accorded President Wilson's demand for suppression of disloyal activity, Congress proved reluctant to pass the security statutes that the Justice Department proposed in June, 1916.[1]

The outbreak of the European war and American army maneuvers on the Mexican border had kept problems of censorship before the Administration since mid-1914.[2] Disclosures in 1914 and 1915 of German and Austrian espionage and sabotage in the United States prompted further re-examination by the Justice Department of federal laws. Administration officials feared that they "had no laws adequate to deal with the insidious methods of internal hostile activities."[3] They believed that the provision of the 1798 Alien Enemies Act which empowered the President to imprison dangerous alien enemies without trial was "the only statute of any real use" which they might employ in case of war.[4] Furthermore, Attorney General Thomas W. Gregory desired legislation {12} adapted to the "new conditions of warfare by propaganda."[5] Hence the legislation he recommended

---

[1] On Dec. 8, 1915, Wilson's Cabinet agreed to co-ordinate the investigatory and intelligence agencies of the various departments and instructed the Attorney General to draft security legislation (New York *Times,* Dec. 9, 1915). For the legislation proposed, see *Report of the Attorney General, 1916,* 12–22.

[2] James R. Mock, *Censorship 1917* (Princeton, 1941), 21, 40.

[3] O'Brian, *Harvard Law Review,* LXVI, 8–9.

[4] *Ibid.*

[5] *Annual Report of the Attorney General, 1918,* 16–17.

in June, 1916, included provisions that would both punish sabotage and curtail freedom of speech and press.[6]

Gregory's proposals of June, 1916, were referred to committee in both houses, and Congress adjourned without acting upon them. The Administration renewed its efforts to bring the security measures to a vote in the special session called in January, 1917. On February 5, statutes to define and punish espionage were finally introduced in the Senate by Lee S. Overman and in the House by Edwin Y. Webb.[7] Although the Senate passed the Webb-Overman bill that month, the House had not brought it to a vote when Congress adjourned on March 4. Thus, when the nation entered into war in April, the passage of the "Espionage Act," an omnibus bill introduced in the new Congress on April 2 and almost identical with the Webb-Overman bill, became one of the first objectives of the Administration.

Two general characteristics of the security measures sponsored by President Wilson must be examined. Firstly, the program rested in large part upon Congressional approval. During the Civil War, President Lincoln had suspended *habeas corpus* and instituted military rule in areas which he deemed endangered by hostile internal activities. Arrest and release of prisoners had been arbitrary, with release generally being ordered when the danger had passed.[8] {13} Wilson was probably aware of

---

[6] See Zechariah Chafee, *Government and Mass Communications* (Chicago, 1947), 447; James R. Mock and Cedric Larson, *Words That Won the War* (Princeton, 1939), 22.

[7] The fate of these early proposals is conveniently summarized in Homer Cummings and Carl MacFarland, *Federal Justice: Chapters in the History of Justice and the Federal Executive* (New York, 1937), 414 ff.

[8] For comparisons of Lincoln's war policies and Wilson's, see J. G. Randall, *The Civil War and Reconstruction* (Boston, 1937), 385–404; W. A. Dunning, "Disloyalty in Two Wars," *American Historical Review*, XXIV (1919), 625–630; J. Malcolm Smith and Cornelius P. Cotter, "The Suppression of Disloyalty in Time of Military

the political pitfalls of arbitrary action,[9] and he requested specific Congressional sanction for most of his security measures. Yet he did not entirely refrain from employing the executive order.

Secondly, the security measures provided for severe punishments. Thus "there was no necessary logical relationship between the intensity and duration of control exercised over particular individuals and the objective need, in security terms, to immobilize them."[10]

The Security Program

In order to judge the Wilson Administration's formulation and implementation of a security program it is necessary to review those executive orders and laws that related to hostile internal activities. Some of these measures—especially the Espionage Act, the Sedition Act, and the Trading-with-the-Enemy Act—have received a great deal of attention from historians.[11] Other measures, which affected fewer persons or which were seldom made the basis of prosecutions, are relatively obscure. Only by viewing the security program in its entirety can one comprehend the exact extent to which the civil liberties of Americans were abridged by federal action during the war years.

1. *Threats against the President Act, February 14, 1917.* The special session of Congress of January–March, 1917, adjourned without passing the Espionage Act. On

---

Danger," a paper presented at the American Political Science Association meeting, Washington, D.C., Sept., 1956 (mimeographed), *passim*.

[9] See Woodrow Wilson, *A History of the American People* (New York, 1902), IV, 260–261.

[10] Smith and Cotter, "The Suppression of Disloyalty," 4.

[11] See, for example, O. A. Hilton, "Public Opinion and Civil Liberties in Wartime, 1917–1919," *Southwestern Social Science Quarterly*, XXVIII (1947), 201–224.

February 14, 1917, however, Congress did pass (with the Attorney General's approval) a bill which punished persons who "knowingly and willfully" made written or spoken statements threatening the life of or bodily harm to the President.[12] The penalty was set at a fine of $1,000 and imprisonment up to five years, a far milder punishment than that provided in the Espionage Act of the following June. {14}

Sixty cases were prosecuted under this act before June, 1918; of these, at least thirty-five resulted in convictions.[13]

2. *Proclamation regarding Alien Enemies, April 6, 1917.* On April 6, the day that the War Resolution was passed by Congress, President Wilson issued a proclamation establishing regulations for the conduct and control of enemy aliens. They were subjected to restrictions of movement, especially in and out of the country, and forbidden to carry or house munitions; to enter the area of a federal or state military post, arsenal, shop, or warehouse; to publish any attack upon the government, the armed forces, or the policies of the United States; and to commit any hostile act against the United States or to render any aid to its enemies. This proclamation was made under the terms of a statute originally passed as part of the Alien Enemies Act of 1798. Under this act all enemy aliens were subject to summary arrest by a federal official.[14]

Also on April 6 the President issued an executive order which charged the Attorney General with the duty of executing the Proclamation.[15] Under this and subsequent

---

[12] 39 U.S. Statutes 919.

[13] *Report of the Attorney General, 1918,* 56; Peterson and Fite, *Opponents of War,* 139, 141.

[14] *Report of the Attorney General, 1917,* 57-59.

[15] *Ibid.,* 59.

executive orders the Justice Department registered enemy aliens and arrested only 6,300, of whom 2,300 were interned by the military as dangerous to the national security.[16]

3. *Confidential Executive Order regarding Federal Employees, April 7, 1917.* On the day following the entry of the United States into the war, President Wilson issued a secret executive order which, had its terms been followed, would have provided the basis for an organized loyalty program affecting every federal employee. Issued at the request of the Civil Service Commission, it empowered department heads to remove any employee deemed a loyalty risk {15} "by reason of his conduct, sympathies, or utterances, or because of other reasons growing out of the war."[17] Such removals might be made summarily, although the Civil Service Commission was empowered to "inspect" dismissals. No estimate can be made of the number of government workers who were affected. It is known, however, that the Civil Service Commission prevented a total of 868 persons from taking examinations for admission to government service, on grounds of questionable loyalty, during the years 1917 to 1921.[18]

---

[16] *Ibid., 1918,* 26; O'Brian, *Harvard Law Review,* LXVI, 11. I make no attempt to list other executive orders which provided for the control of enemy aliens. For a summary of Presidential proclamations and Justice Department actions, see *Report of the Attorney General, 1918,* 27 ff. For a statement concerning the execution of Presidential orders regarding enemy aliens, see chapter IV, "Justice Department," *infra.* See also Peterson and Fite, *Opponents of War,* 81–86.

[17] The full text is reproduced in Paul P. Van Riper, *History of the United States Civil Service* (Evanston, 1958), 266.

[18] *Ibid.,* 267. The New York *Times* reported on July 6, 1917, that "suspected individuals have been subjected to strict surveillance and discharges from public service among this class have been frequent." In the case of the dismissal of one postal clerk in St. Louis for statements such as "To hell with the Allies," there is no evidence of review by the Civil Service Commission (A. S. Burleson to Wilson, Aug. 6, 1917, File VI, 4181, Wilson Papers). I have

This order was enacted by Congress as a provision of the Sedition Act of May 16, 1918, but in revised form: the discharge of an employee was not, after that date, subject to review by the Civil Service Commission.[19]

4. *Creation of the Committee on Public Information, April 14, 1917.* On April 14, 1917, President Wilson under his emergency powers created the Committee on Public Information and assigned funds for its operation from the President's emergency reserve. This action was recommended by members of the Cabinet. On the previous day Secretaries Baker, Daniels, and Lansing had written to Wilson stating, "It is our opinion that ... censorship and publicity can be joined in honesty and with profit, and we recommend a Committee on Public Information."[20] Wilson appointed George Creel, a progressive journalist, to be chairman of the C.P.I. Baker, Daniels, and Lansing were to be the other members of the committee.

The C.P.I. became the Administration's official information and {16} publicity agency, and in this field it made its mark. Until the passage of the Espionage Act, Creel organized the voluntary self-censorship which the press had accepted; after the Espionage Act became law, the censorship functions of the C.P.I. became insignificant. Lansing had absolutely no confidence in Creel, believing him to be too liberal, and soon withdrew from the committee. Daniels writes that Lansing refused to serve because he "wanted the censorship to be like that of Europe, and shut off all the news."[21]

---

searched for other evidence of dismissals in the National Civil Service Reform League Papers, Regional History Collection, Cornell University Library, but without success. See note 21 of this chapter.

[19] 40 U.S. Statutes 555.

[20] 20 Baker, *Life and Letters,* VII, 20.

[21] Josephus Daniels, *The Wilson Era: Years of War and After* (Chapel Hill, 1946), 227. Creel himself disliked the idea of censor-

As a propaganda agency, the C.P.I. did its work well—all too well, perhaps. For Creel mobilized journalists, artists, writers, advertisers, and professors in a campaign that often seemed geared to persuade the American people that every German soldier was a violent beast; that spies and saboteurs lurked behind every bush; that conscription, bond sales, and "liberty cabbage" were the greatest national blessings since the Bill of Rights; and that Russian Bolsheviks were merely German agents.[22]

The C.P.I. must receive much credit for building a spirit of confidence and support for the war effort.[23] Yet, as a result of its campaigning, the loyalty of the innocent enemy alien was undoubtedly impugned, and excesses were probably encouraged. At {17} times the C.P.I. proved itself capable of drowning out the voices of those who took a more balanced and judicious view of the disloyalty question. Writing shortly after the war, Special Assistant Attorney General John Lord O'Brian stated: "No other one cause contributed so much to the oppres-

---

ship and wrote to Wilson that "the need was for expression, not repression" (quoted in James E. Pollard, *The Presidents and the Press* [New York, 1947], 659). Lansing created a stir in the nation's press when, on May 8, 1917, he announced that "any subordinate giving out information conveying a criticism of the department's policies would be dismissed" (Baker, *Life and Letters,* VII, 57).

[22] See C.P.I. War Information Series, No. 20, "The German-Bolshevik Conspiracy" [the Sisson Documents]; Mock and Larson, *Words That Won the War,* 64 (poster reading "German Agents are everywhere. . ."), 65 (poster reading "Halt the Hun").

[23] I make no attempt at a definitive judgment of Creel. See, however, Robert L. Morlan, *Political Prairie Fire: The Nonpartisan League, 1915–1922* (Minneapolis, 1955), 166–167, 181–182, for an example of Creel's efforts to clear the Nonpartisan League of charges of disloyalty broadcast by its conservative political enemies. See also Hilton, *Southwestern Soc. Sci. Quar.,* XXVIII, 206; Peterson and Fite, *Opponents of War,* 18; Mock and Larson, *Words That Won the War,* ch. i; Creel, *The War, the World, and Wilson* (New York, 1920).

sion of innocent men as the systematic and indiscriminate agitation against what was claimed to be an all-pervasive system of German espionage."[24] The C.P.I. was a foremost initiator of such agitation.

5. *Executive Order relating to Cable and Land Telegraph Lines, April 28, 1917.* An executive order of April 28, 1917, also involved censorship: it broadened the censorship authority of the Navy Department which had originally been established over radio stations in August, 1914, by giving the Navy control over submarine cables. Also, the War Department was given charge of censoring messages sent out of the country on telephone and land telegraph lines. In actual practice the major effect of this order was the censorship established over messages outgoing on cable lines, for these included reports on American news to foreign newspapers. Unlike the newspaper censorship functions which were exercised by the Postmaster General, this cable censorship was discontinued after June, 1919.[25]

6. *The Espionage Act, June 15, 1917.* When, on the evening of April 2, 1917, President Wilson asked Congress to recognize a state of war between the United States and Germany, he included in his indictment of Germany the activities of German agents in the United States: "From the very outset of the present war [Germany] has filled our unsuspecting communities and even our offices of government with spies and set criminal intrigues everywhere afoot against our national unity of counsel, our peace within and without, our industries and our commerce."[26] Of the German-born, Wilson assured Congress that most of them were loyal Americans. Hopeful that

---

[24] "Civil Liberty in War Time," 65th Cong., 3rd Sess., Senate Doc. 434 (Washington, 1919), 5.

[25] Mock, *Censorship, 1917,* 79, 81, 93.

[26] *Congress. Rec.,* LV (65th Cong., Spec. Sess.), 104.

they would thenceforth stand solidly behind the government in the war with Germany, Wilson issued a stern warning {18} to those who would not: "If there should be disloyalty, it will be dealt with with a firm hand of stern repression; but, if it lifts its head at all, it will lift it only here and there without countenance except from a lawless and malignant few."[27]

Immediately after the conclusion of the President's War Message, Representative Webb and Senator Charles A. Culberson introduced bills which would provide the President with the instrument of "stern repression" which he had requested. Nine weeks later, these bills, much amended, were to become the Espionage Act of June 15, 1917.

The debate on the Espionage Act was protracted and often muddled and confusing. Most of the discussion was prompted by the universal objection of the American press to a press-censorship provision which the President demanded. (Wilson wished to have Congress provide for a $10,000 fine and ten years' imprisonment for any person convicted of publishing such information as would be declared by a Presidential proclamation to be useful or possibly useful to the enemy.[28]) Wilson insisted that such censorship would be "absolutely necessary to the public safety."[29] Throughout the debate Wilson emphasized the importance of censorship from the standpoint of military needs.[30] Despite the President's firm stand in the face of increasing and formidable opposition, the censorship provision was defeated in the

---

[27] *Ibid.*

[28] Letter to Webb, in New York *Times,* May 23, 1917.

[29] *Ibid.*

[30] Mock, *Censorship, 1917,* 30 ff.

House on May 31 by a vote of 184 to 144.[31] The Senate did not bring it to a vote.[32]

Once Wilson had been defeated on the censorship, press criticism and, indeed, press notice of the Espionage Act suddenly ceased.[33] If it is true that "after its elimination, a majority of the national lawmakers apparently believed that the bill could not be {19} used to suppress critical opinion,"[34] then these Congressmen were mistaken. For two of the twelve titles of the act, as passed, bore directly upon freedom of speech.

Section 3 of Title I provided the punishment of a $10,000 fine or imprisonment for up to twenty years or both, for those who, when the United States is at war,

> shall willfully make or convey false reports or false statements with intent to interfere with the operation or success of the military or naval forces of the United States or to promote the success of its enemies; and whoever, when the United States is at war, shall willfully cause or attempt to cause insubordination, disloyalty, mutiny, or refusal of duty in the military or naval forces of the United States, or shall willfully obstruct the recruitment or enlistment service of the United States.[35]

With later amendments, this section was to be used by the Department of Justice to prosecute more than 2,000 cases. At least 1,055 citizens were convicted under

---

[31] Although Burleson was seen in the lobbies working for the passage of censorship, 37 Democrats voted against it; 11 Republicans voted with the Administration (New York *Times,* June 1, 1917).

[32] *Ibid.,* June 2, 1917. For an earlier vote, however, see *ibid.,* May 13, 1917.

[33] Mock and Larson, *Words That Won the War,* 41.

[34] Peterson and Fite, *Opponents of War,* 16. The President specifically denied that the Espionage Act would be used to suppress criticism of the Administration (letter to Arthur Brisbane, April 25, 1917, Wilson Papers).

[35] 40 U.S. Statutes 219.

its terms, among them more than 150 I.W.W. leaders, at least one Senatorial nominee (J. A. Peterson, Republican, of Minnesota), and Eugene V. Debs, the choice for President of 900,000 Americans in 1912.[36] Despite the menace that these persons allegedly represented, not one bona fide spy or saboteur was convicted during World War I.[37]

Title XII vested the Postmaster General with vast powers for the suppression of critical opinion. Any matter violating the act or "advocating or urging treason, insurrection, or forcible resistance to any law of the United States" was declared non-mailable; a maximum penalty of five years imprisonment or a $5,000 fine, or both, was established for attempting to use the mails for the distribution of such matter.[38] Thus Albert S. Burleson was awarded virtually dictatorial control over the effective circulation of the {20} "subsidiary press" of the nation.[39] He proved to be neither a temperate nor a benevolent dictator.

7. *The Trading-with-the-Enemy Act, October 6, 1917.* On October 6, 1917, the censorship powers of the Postmaster General were further enlarged by the terms of the Trading-with-the-Enemy Act. Burleson had already demonstrated that one of his primary interests in enforcing the Espionage Act was to crush the pacifist, anti-Administration, left-wing press. Thus the members of Congress must have known full well the illiberal spirit in

---

[36] See Appendix, *infra*. The amendments were embodied in the "Sedition Act," discussed later in this chapter.

[37] John Lord O'Brian *National Security and Individual Freedom* (Cambridge, 1955), 49–50.

[38] 40 U.S. Statutes 231.

[39] The phrase "subsidiary press" is used to refer to those periodicals with relatively limited circulations and generally meager financial resources, appealing to special audiences such as foreign-language groups or small minority political groups.

which new powers would be employed. Yet the Trading-with-the-Enemy Act required foreign-language newspapers to submit to the Post Office Department for approval before mailing literal translations of all news and editorial articles which contained material on the government, the belligerent powers and their policies, or conduct of the war. Should the President be satisfied that a particular newspaper was loyal, then he might issue a permit which would allow publication without the filing of translations.[40] In practice, this duty devolved upon Burleson.

This act placed a great financial strain upon the type of newspapers that could least afford it. Furthermore, it involved damaging delays in publication. As a result, practically every one of the German-language papers by mid-1918 was forced either to adopt a progovernment editorial policy or to maintain a judicious silence on war questions.[41]

Section 3 of the Trading-with-the-Enemy Act, with Title VII of the Espionage Act, served as the statutory basis for the first federal censorship board in the nation's history. The section provided that

> whenever, during the present war, the President shall deem that the public safety demands it, he may cause to be censored under such rules {21} and regulations as he may from time to time establish, communications by mail, cable, radio, or other means of transmission passing between the United States and any foreign country.[42]

---

[40] 40 U.S. Statutes 425–426.

[41] Wittke, *German-Americans,* 135–139, 173–174. Urging Wilson to veto the bill, one civil rights group asserted, "Postmaster General's reported attitude means total abolition during war of entire radical and most of labor press" (National Civil Liberties Bureau to Wilson, Sept. 26, 1917, Wilson Papers).

[42] U.S. Statutes 412–413.

The punishment for any person employing a code or other device in an attempt to evade this censorship would be a fine of $10,000 or not more than ten years' imprisonment, or both.

Thus the Administration was empowered to continue the radio and cable censorship already instituted; private mail leaving the country was to be subjected to the censor's scrutiny; and penalties were provided for evasion. The President undoubtedly stood on firm ground when he urged Congress to provide for censorship of messages sent abroad; the provision concerning foreign-language publications was quite another matter.[43]

8. *Executive Order Establishing the Board of Censorship, October 12, 1917.* President Wilson lost no time in concluding that "the public safety demanded" scrutiny of communications leaving the country. Only six days after he approved the Trading-with-the-Enemy Act, he created a Board of Censorship to handle such censorship. The board was to consist of representatives of the War and Navy Departments, the Post Office Department, the War Trade Board, and the chairman of the Committee on Public Information.[44] Yet through the power of the purse Postmaster General Burleson and his assistant, Otto Praeger, assumed practical control of the board and its policies.[45] Thus Wilson further strengthened the hand of Burleson, who forthwith ordered examination of the private letters of many anti-interventionist progressives. The board also gathered information concerning "the Bolsheviki, Industrial Workers of the World, Socialists,

---

[43] See Wittke, *German-Language Press, passim.*

[44] Mock, *Censorship, 1917,* 53.

[45] "Report of Special Committee ré Censorship of Mail, April 23, 1918," in File VI, 3856, Wilson Papers. The President approved of Burleson's assumption of control over this phase of censorship despite the objections of Creel and others (Wilson to R. L. Maddox April 29, 1918, *ibid.*).

and other organizations whose aims are antagonistic to this government," in the words of one Seattle Censor.[46] {22}

In May, 1918, Theodore Roosevelt informed a private correspondent, stationed with the Army in France, that he dared not comment upon the Administration's conduct of the war, for he could not be certain what the censors might open![47]

9. *The Sabotage Act, April 20, 1918.* Even though the Espionage Act was designed to protect the country from an imagined network of saboteurs and spies, Congress did not pass a sabotage law until April 20, 1918.[48] One year earlier the Attorney General had recommended passage of a law providing punishment for "malicious destruction or injury to property, no matter how essential the property might be to the conduct of the War."[49] Given the sweeping language of this statute, it is well that a man of Gregory's and not of Burleson's temperament was in charge of its enforcement.

10. *The Sedition Act, May 16, 1918.* Traditional civil liberties were severely circumscribed by January, 1918, as these statutes and executive orders took effect. In that month, however, Representative Webb once again stepped forward in the House to defend the nation by proposing further limitations upon the freedom of her citizens. He offered a bill which appealed to those super-patriots who yearned for extreme repression, a bill designed to frighten and ultimately silence many Americans who favored a restoration of traditional freedom of expression. Webb's bill, known as the Sedition Act, took the

---

[46] Quoted in Mock, *Censorship, 1917,* 130. The work of the Censorship Board is discussed *ibid.,* 110–130.

[47] Letter to Willard Straight, May 16, 1918, Straight Papers.

[48] 40 U.S. Statutes 533.

[49] *Report of the Attorney General, 1918,* 18.

form of amendments to the Espionage Act; it became law on May 16, 1918.[50]

High Administration officials had long been demanding an act against "dangerous utterances." For example, in a Flag Day address in June, 1917, President Wilson condemned as disloyal those Americans who opposed intervention:

> Do you not now understand the new intrigue, the intrigue for peace, and why the masters of Germany do not hesitate to use any agency that promises to effect their purpose, the deceit of the nations? ... They are employing liberals in their enterprise. They are using men, in Germany and without, as their spokesmen ... — socialists, the leaders of labor, the thinkers they have hitherto sought to silence. ... That {23} Government has many spokesmen here, in places high and low. *They have learned discretion. They keep within the law. It is opinion they utter, now, not sedition.*
>
> They proclaim the liberal purposes of their masters; declare this a foreign war which can touch America with no danger to either her lands or her institutions. [They] appeal to our ancient tradition of isolation in the politics of the nations; and seek to undermine the Government with false professions of loyalty to its principles. But they will make no headway. The false betray themselves always in every accent. It is only friends and partisans of the German Government whom we have already identified who utter these *thinly disguised disloyalties.*[51]

On April 16, while the House was debating the Sedition Act, the Attorney General made public a letter which he had written to Representative Gilbert A. Currie earlier that month. Currie had suggested to Gregory that "our Government authorities are dealing too leniently with

---

[50] 40 U.S. Statutes 553-554.

[51] Address of June 14, 1917 *Congress. Rec.*, LV (65th Cong., 1st Sess.), Appendix, 334. Italics added.

spies and dangerous enemies within our confines." Gregory replied, "If such a feeling does exist, it is mainly caused by the lack of Federal statutes and not by any lack of activity upon the part of prosecuting officials." In particular Gregory deplored "the lack of laws relating to disloyal utterances."[52]

At the time that Gregory affixed his signature to the letter, more than 250 offenders were in prison after conviction under the terms of the Espionage Act. Yet justice Department officials believed that "some of the most dangerous types of propaganda were either made from good motives or else that the traitorous motive was not provable."[53] Gregory concluded his letter by stating, "It is earnestly {24} hoped that Congress ... will give the government adequate weapons with which to prevent the spread of flagrant disloyalty." He recommended specifically that Congress make punishable attempts both to obstruct the recruiting service and to interfere with the

---

[52] Quoted in *Official Bulletin,* April 16, 1918. (The *Official Bulletin* was published daily by the Committee on Public Information May 10, 1917 to March 31, 1919, and is an invaluable source for Administration policy, often overlooked by students of this period.)

[53] *Report of the Attorney General, 1918,* 18. Writing to Representative Webb during the debates, O'Brian asserted that in many cases of dangerous propaganda "few facts are stated; the facts which are stated are generally true and it is difficult to disprove good motives" (New York *Times,* April 25, 1918). At the time that Gregory wrote to Currie, Vincente Balbas was in prison serving eight years for denouncing conscription of Puerto Ricans who bad declined to accept American citizenship; J. O. Bentall was serving a five-year sentence imposed for speeches delivered during his campaign for governor in Minnesota; and Conrad Kornemann was awaiting sentence in Sioux Falls, South Dakota, having been convicted for denouncing the Liberty Loan in a private letter (National Civil Liberties Bureau, "War-time Prosecutions and Mob Violence" [pamphlet, New York, 1918], 12–13). Gregory clearly had mixed feelings about many convictions under the Espionage Act (Gregory to Wilson, Aug. 22, 1917, May 14, 1918, Wilson Papers; Gregory to T. U. Taylor, April 15, 1918, T. W. Gregory Papers, Library of Congress).

sale of war bonds. The Senate judiciary Committee defined eight new offenses, along with Gregory's recommendations, in drafting the Sedition Act.[54] The offenses included uttering, printing, writing, or publishing any disloyal, profane, scurrilous, or abusive language intended to cause contempt, scorn, contumely or disrepute as regards the form of government of the United States, or the Constitution, or the flag, or the uniform of the Army or Navy, or any language intended to incite resistance to the United States or to promote the cause of its enemies; urging any curtailment of production of any thing necessary to the prosecution of the war with intent to hinder its prosecution; advocating, teaching, defending, or suggesting the doing of any of these acts; and words or acts supporting or favoring the cause of any country at war with the United States, or opposing the cause of the United States in time of war.[55]

The penalty provided was a $10,000 fine or not more than twenty years' imprisonment, or both.[56] The law was so broad and vague in its language that, in the words of John Lord O'Brian, it "covered in all degrees of conduct and speech, serious and trifling alike, and, in the popular mind, gave the dignity of treason to what were often neighborhood quarrels or barroom brawls."[57]

The Sedition Act also enlarged the censorship functions of the Postmaster General. "Upon evidence satisfactory to him," the Postmaster General was empowered to refuse to deliver mail to any {25} individual or business concern employing the mails in violation of the statute. He was to order letters which he deemed undeliverable to be returned to the sender with the phrase "Mail to this

---

[54] See Zechariah Chafee, *Freedom of Speech* (New York, 1920), 44.

[55] 40 U.S. Statutes 553-554.

[56] See Mock and Larson, *Words That Won the War*, 34.

[57] "Civil Liberty in War Time," 18.

address undeliverable under the Espionage Act" stamped upon the envelope.[58] Thus the Postmaster General was empowered to damage or destroy the business or reputation of any American citizen.[59]

The New York *Times* reported that on the day the bill came to a vote Democratic floor managers were active in the House lobbies. Justice Department officials asserted that vigorous enforcement of the act, should it be passed, would remove the causes of mob violence and "vigilante justice."[60] The Senate vote found the Democrats almost unanimously in favor of the bill; the House vote was marked by only one negative vote, although 46 were paired, and 134 did not vote.[61] Gregory approved the definition of new offenses incorporated into the Sedition Act. "With the use of a reasonable amount of discretion and caution on the part of law officers there should be no abuse of the powers conferred," he declared.[62] Yet he doubted the constitutionality of the censorship powers granted to the Postmaster General. Fearful that judicial powers wielded by an administrative official would have "an indirect but far reaching inhibitory effect upon the right of free public discussion," Gregory

---

[58] Carl B. Swisher, *American Constitutional Development* (Boston, 1943), 606.

[59] 40 U.S. Statutes 554. Ironically the progressives in Congress had previously been the foremost advocates of measures denying use of the mails as a punitive device. For example, it had frequently been suggested that monopolistic corporations be denied the use of the mails (Lindsay Rogers, *The Postal Power of Congress: A Study in Constitutional Expansion* [Baltimore, 1916], 162, 180). In December, 1915 a bill was introduced to forbid use of the mails to any publication containing matter denouncing any race, creed, or religion; one newspaper condemned it as a Jewish-Catholic attempt to muzzle the press (Aurora, Missouri, *Menace*, Dec. 25, 1915 clipping in Wilson Papers).

[60] New York *Times,* May 8, 1918.

[61] *Ibid.,* May 5, 8, 1918.

[62] Letter to Wilson, May 14, 1918, Wilson Papers.

left the decision to Wilson.[63] The President {26} chose to sign the bill, and the Sedition Act became law on May 16, 1918.

11. *The Alien Act, October 16, 1918.* Having enacted a sedition act in the spirit of 1798, Congress now devoted itself to drafting an alien law. In February, 1917, an immigration act had been passed over the President's veto which was designed to protect the country from the pernicious danger of radicalism. The 1917 act (1) reaffirmed the exclusion of anarchists, first established by law in 1903; (2) removed the three-year limitation for deportation of those who had entered by falsely swearing that they were not anarchists; (3) introduced the principle of guilt by association into American immigration law by excluding any person "who is a member of or affiliated with any organization entertaining or teaching disbelief in or opposition to organized government,"[64] and making such persons subject to deportation; and (4) required a literacy test of such persons.[65] In returning the bill without his signature, President Wilson stated, "In most of the provisions of the bill I should be very glad to

---

[63] *Ibid.* Gregory asserted later in 1918 that among the Espionage Act offenders were "men and women who have not the slightest sympathy with Germany, whose loyalty in so far as they have national loyalty is exclusively for the United States, who are intensely sincere. . . and are guilty of no secret action against the interests of this country. . . [yet] who give public voice to sentiments obstructive of the war effort" (letter to Wilson, Aug. 21, 1918, Wilson Papers).

[64] U.S. Department of Justice, Immigration and Naturalization Service, *Laws Applicable to Immigration* and *Nationality* (Washington, 1953) 370. Compare William Preston, "The Ideology and Techniques of Repression, 1903-1933," in Harvey Goldberg, ed., *American Radicals: Some Problems and Personalities* (New York, 1957), 254; hereinafter cited as "Ideology and Techniques." See also Milton R. Konvitz, *Civil Rights in Immigration* (Ithaca, 1953), 28.

[65] For this act, see *Laws Applicable to Immigration and Nationality*, 318 ff.

concur," but explained that he could not accept the principle of the literacy test.⁶⁶ It was passed over his veto.

The President did, however, sign the Act of October 16, 1918. This act empowered the government to deport, upon the warrant of the Secretary of Labor, "any alien who, at any time after entering the United States, is found to have been at the time of entry, or *to have become thereafter*," a member of any anarchist organization.⁶⁷
{27}

The significance of the Alien Act should not be underestimated. Its passage reflects the fact that insistent wartime attacks against disloyalty had generated in Congress a desire to protect the government from an alleged anarchist menace. This law arose out of the same impulse to eliminate the dissenter, to remove the dissatisfied, that prompted former Ambassador James W. Gerard to remark in November, 1917, "We should hog-tie every disloyal German American, feed every pacifist raw meat, and hang every traitor to a lamppost to insure success in this War."⁶⁸

In June, 1917, President Wilson had warned those who opposed the war: "For us there is but one choice. We have made it. Woe be to the man or group of men that seeks to stand in our way in this day of high resolution...."⁶⁹ The Alien Act was part and parcel of the program which Congress devised to eliminate those who sought to stand in the way.

The implications of the Alien Act were not to become evident until 1919 and 1920. It was the capstone of a long succession of laws which removed those legal guarantees

---

⁶⁶ *Public Papers*, IV, 420.

⁶⁷ U.S. Statutes 1012. Italics added.

⁶⁸ Quoted in American Civil Liberties Union, "Who May Advocate the Use of Force?" (pamphlet, New York, 1922), 2.

⁶⁹ Flag Day Address, June 14, 1917, *Public Papers,* V, 67.

traditionally enjoyed by Americans against the arbitrary actions of hysterical or irresponsible government officials. And it was to provide the legal basis for Attorney General A. Mitchell Palmers notorious and ruthless antiradical crusade, "the greatest executive restriction of personal liberty in the history of this country."[70]

"A firm hand of stern repression"

By means of these laws and executive orders President Wilson acquired the "firm hand of stern repression" which he had demanded in his War Message. Several characteristics of the security program are of particular importance and should be noted in closing:

1. The severely punitive character of the legislation has already been discussed. Violations of the Espionage and Sedition Acts, under which the bulk of prosecutions were instituted, were penalized {28} by as much as a $10,000 fine, imprisonment up to twenty years, or both.

2. The Espionage and Sedition Acts were to be operative "in time of war." Thus, probably unwittingly, Congress left the door open for the Executive to continue enforcement of these acts should a technical state of war continue to exist following the conclusion of an armistice. The Administration did prosecute under these statutes after November 11, 1918, despite the fact that Congress clearly expressed its desire to put an end to postwar censorship and prosecutions under the Espionage and Sedition Acts. In May, 1920, Wilson vetoed a bill which would have terminated these statutes. He thereby deliberately confounded the legislators' intention to curb the extraordinary powers which they had delegated to him during an emergency.[71]

---

[70] Zechariah Chafee, *Free Speech in the United States* (Cambridge, 1941), 214.

[71] Swisher, *American Constitutional Development,* 686. The bill referred to here is not the bill which Wilson vetoed on May 28 and

3. As Attorney General Gregory wrote, these measures were "necessarily framed in general language," and prosecution generally involved "not only great discrimination of judgement, but the fundamental question of the rights of free speech and political agitation."[72] A great burden fell upon the shoulders of the President, the Attorney General, and the Postmaster General: their decisions were to be a deciding factor in the maintenance of civil liberties, for the courts proved willing to interpret the repressive statutes most broadly.[73] The following chapters comprise an attempt to review and judge the decisions and policies of these high federal officials.

---

which would have ended the technical state of war. The bill in question would merely have put an end to these extraordinary delegated powers.

[72] *Report of the Attorney General, 1918*, 21.

[73] For judicial decisions, see Chafee, *Free Speech, passim,* and Hilton, *Southwestern Soc. Sci. Quar.,* XXVIII, 346–361, 214–224.

III • Censorship

IN THIS age of relativist history one seldom encounters unanimity of opinion such as exists concerning the censorship practices of Wilson's Postmaster General.

Professor Carl Brent Swisher has written that Burleson "exercised his power of censorship with a high hand, excluding from the mails publications which only by farfetched lines of reasoning could be held in violation of the statute."[1] Historian John Morton Blum states that "the myopic Postmaster General"[2] banned publications from the mails "on flimsy pretexts and without explanation.... The President's secretary discovered that Burleson's standards of censorship were more severe than those of the Army."[3] The late Zechariah Chafee wrote that "the nation had been led on by its panic-stricken fear of adverse opinion to abandon one national tradition after another. Everyone agreed that freedom of speech meant the absence of previous administrative restraint on political discussion—and the Postmaster General was allowed to establish a whimsical censorship of the political press."[4] John Lord O'Brian concurs, stating that postal officials worked at cross-purposes with himself and Gregory.[5] {30}

These judgments of the administration of censorship are not materially different from contemporaneous criticisms, leveled from many different quarters. For exam-

---

[1] *American Constitutional Development*, 610.

[2] *Woodrow Wilson and the Politics of Morality* (Boston, 1956), 143.

[3] *Midwest Journal*, III, 49.

[4] *Free Speech*, 272.

[5] *Harvard Law Review*, LXVI, 14.

ple, Theodore Roosevelt wrote in May, 1918: "During the past year the action of the Administration, taken largely through the Post-Office Department, has been such as to render it a matter of some danger for any man, and especially newspapermen, to speak the truth, if that truth be unpleasant to the governmental authorities at Washington."[6] From the other end of the political spectrum Upton Sinclair wrote to Wilson, "It is hard to draw the line, Mr. President, as to the amount of ignorance permitted to a government official; but Mr. Burleson is assuredly on the wrong side of any line that could be drawn by anyone."[7] In September, 1918, the New York *World*, regarded as an Administration newspaper, remarked that "the bureaucrats of the Post-Office Department ... seem determined to set up an intellectual reign of terror in the United States."[8]

Burleson's censorship policies might have been curbed in either of two ways: the force of public opinion might have compelled moderation, or the President might have controlled his subordinate's actions.

In *The Federalist,* No. 84, Alexander Hamilton asked: "What is the liberty of the press? Who can give it any definition which would not leave the utmost latitude for evasion? ... [It] must altogether depend on public opinion, and on the general spirit of the people and of the government." In the electric atmosphere of an America which suddenly found itself involved in war in 1917, the general spirit of the people was not a tolerant one. Ugly intolerance and insistence upon conformity took many forms: the German language was eliminated from the

---

[6] Elting Morison, ed., *The Letters of Theodore Roosevelt,* vol. VIII "The Days of Armageddon, 1914–1919" (Cambridge, 1954), 1323.

[7] Letter of Oct., 1917, quoted in Peterson and Fite, *Opponents of War,* 100.

[8] Sept. 22, 1918, in a National Civil Liberties Bureau reprint (no title), Cornell University Library.

curriculum in thousands of public schools; in many towns self-appointed "assessors" coerced citizens and aliens alike by establishing Liberty Loan quotas; reactionary elements, acting in the name of patriotism, used violence against {31} labor-union leaders and strikers as "an orgy of hatred" gripped the nation.[9]

With public opinion in this frenzied state, it was unlikely that political pressure would force Burleson to abandon abusive policies. Hence the responsibility for restraining the Postmaster General fell upon the shoulders of the President. Wilson realized this, and throughout the war years he exchanged many letters with Burleson on questions of censorship.[10] The story of Burleson's abuse of his powers and his relationship with the President merits examination.

A Capricious Censorship[11]

The Espionage Act and the Sedition Act empowered the Postmaster General to ban from the mails only matter which was in violation of the statutes. There was, however, no specific provision for the handling of subsequent issues of a publication once banned.

Thus Burleson went far beyond the intention of the legislation when, in the summer of 1917, he ruled that at his discretion any publication might be denied the privilege of the second-class mails.[12] In the cases of the New

---

[9] Handlin, *American People in 20th Century,* 124. See also Arthur S. Link, *American Epoch: A History of the United States since the 1890's* (New York, 1953), 216; Peterson and Fite, *Opponents of War, passim;* J. Weinstein, "Anti-War Sentiment and the Socialist Party, 1917-1918," *Political Science Quarterly,* LXXIV (1959), 215-239.

[10] See Baker, *Life and Letters,* vols. VII-VIII, *passim;* James E. Pollard, *The Presidents and the Press* (New York, 1947), 659–691.

[11] The phrase is from Link, *American Epoch,* 214.

[12] New York *Times,* July 6, 1917.

York *Masses* and the Milwaukee *Leader*, Burleson decreed that he might revoke the second-class privileges of any publication which had had one issue banned on the grounds that "since the magazine had skipped a number ... it was no longer a periodical."[13] Burleson took this action under the terms of the Classification Act of 1879, which ruled that publications "issued at stated intervals" were eligible for second-class mailing privileges. Burleson claimed that, should one issue be declared non-mailable, then the publication ceased to be issued at such {32} "stated intervals."[14] The lower courts upheld Burleson's construction of the statute; and in 1921 the Supreme Court reviewed the question, ruling in favor of the government.[15] Explaining his policy, Burleson wrote that "it was found necessary to revoke the second-class mail privilege of some publications for the reason that their contents consisted more or less of matter which was non-mailable under the espionage law."[16] Burleson used censorship as a bludgeon with which to destroy the left-wing press.[17] By September, 1918, he had denied the second-class mailing privilege to some twenty-two Socialist newspapers.[18] Among the publications barred from the mails were the *Freeman's Journal*, for reprinting Thomas Jefferson's statements favoring independence for Ireland; the *Irish World*, for predicting that "Palestine would not be a Jewish kingdom"; and a National Civil

---

[13] Chafee, *Freedom of Speech*, 107.

[14] Chafee, *Government and Mass Communications*, 294–295.

[15] *Ibid.*

[16] *Report of the Postmaster General, 1918*, 46.

[17] See Villard, *Fighting Years*, 327.

[18] Hilton, *Southwestern* Soc. *Sci. Quar.*, XXVIII, 353; Lindsay Rogers, "Freedom of Press in the United States," *Living Age*, CCXCVIII (1918), 770.

Liberties Bureau pamphlet which deplored mob violence.[19]

Burleson did not always limit his attacks to the subsidiary press. The September 14, 1918, issue of the influential liberal magazine, the *Nation*, was barred from the mails. Editor Oswald Garrison Villard was informed that publication of an article criticizing Samuel Gompers was the reason for suspension of mailing privileges. "Mr. Gompers has rendered inestimable services to this government during the war in holding union labor in line," Post Office Solicitor William Lamar stated. "While this war is on, we are not going to allow any newspaper in this country to attack him."[20] Probably because of Wilson's intervention, the ban was rescinded and the *Nation* was not subjected to further harassment.[21] Commenting upon this affair, the New York *World* concluded: "To say that this is asinine would be gross flattery; yet the episode is wholly {33} characteristic of bureaucratic methods in dealing with public discussion of issues relating to the war.... This heresy-hunting, this witch-burning, this lynching of ideas, goes on everywhere."[22]

Burleson did all he could to detract from the effectiveness of the National Civil Liberties Bureau, a new organization (originally a subcommittee of the American Union Against Militarism) devoted to protection of the rights of conscience.[23] Also, the Postmaster General twice

---

[19] A.C.L.U., "Who May Advocate the Use of Force?" Chafee, *Free Speech,* 99; Mock, *Censorship, 1917,* 145 ff.

[20] Villard, *Fighting Years,* 355.

[21] *Ibid.,* 356; Peterson and Fite, *Opponents of War,* 100.

[22] Sept. 22, 1918, N.C.L.B. reprint (no title).

[23] Barton Bean, "Pressure for Freedom: The American Civil Liberties Union" (Ph.D. dissertation, Cornell University, 1954), 43. In addition to this full-scale history, see Lucille Milner, *The Education of an American Liberal* (New York, 1954), and Walter Nelles, *A Liberal in Wartime* (New York, 1940), for the experiences of Milner

warned the *New Republic* that it would be excluded from the mails if it published the Bureau's advertisements appealing for donations and volunteer help.[24] On another occasion Burleson is reported to have detained Bureau literature in transit without notifying the Bureau officers of that fact.[25]

The Subsidiary Press

Many foreign-language newspapers fell victim to Burleson and Lamar. In announcing the conditions which would rule the issuance of permits under the Trading-with-the-Enemy Act, Burleson stated, "We shall take great care not to let criticism which is personally or politically offensive to the Administration affect our action. But if newspapers go so far as to impugn the motives of the Government and thus encourage insubordination, they will be dealt with severely." Burleson spelled out very precisely his extraordinary notion as to what constituted disloyalty:

> For instance, papers may not say that the Government is controlled by Wall Street or munitions manufacturers, or any other special interests. . . . We will not tolerate campaigns against conscription, enlistments, sale of securities [Liberty Bonds], or revenue collections. We will not permit the publication or circulation of anything hampering the war's prosecution or attacking improperly our allies.[26] {34}

In the face of this code many papers suspended publication, while others adopted a policy of refraining from

---

and Albert DeSilver, both early members of the N.C.L.B. (which was succeeded by the A.C.L.U. in 1920).

[24] Milner, *Education of a Liberal,* 68. Compare with Nelles, *Liberal in Wartime,* 140–141.

[25] Nelles, *Liberal in Wartime,* 146–147.

[26] New York *Times,* Oct. 10, 1917.

editorial comment.[27] For example, after a hearing before Burleson in October, 1917, Abraham Cahan, the distinguished editor of the Yiddish *Daily Forward*, announced that "the paper will henceforth publish war news without comment and will not criticize the allies, in order to avoid suspension of mailing privileges."[28] A vivid expression of the principles under which Burleson exercised his censorship of the press is found in an open letter, published in response to a local postmaster's complaint that some residents of his community declined to purchase savings stamps for religious reasons. Postal officials stated that "when in its wisdom and its patriotism the majority has spoken in legal and proper manner, every loyal member of the minority should become one with the majority." Those who refuse to conform, they asserted, do not deserve the protection of the law.[29]

In the months which followed the Armistice of 1918, the United States remained technically at war, and Burleson adapted his interpretation of the minority's obligation to conform. The Postmaster General employed his continuing emergency powers under the Espionage and Sedition Acts to deal with what he deemed a new menace:

> The character of the disloyal and seditious matter found in the mails since the signing of the armistice has differed materially from that with which the De-

---

[27] Peterson and Fite, *Opponents of War,* 99.

[28] New York *Times,* Oct. 7, 1917.

[29] *Official Bulletin,* March 28, 1918. Administration officials maintained the fiction that no legislation had been enacted for the suppression of foreign-language newspapers and that protests against attacks on the foreign-language press were therefore incomprehensible (Tumulty to Henry Pfeiffer, May 31, 1918, File VI, 4182, Wilson Papers).

> partment dealt during the prosecution of the war. It is now of a radical, revolutionary type.[30] ...
>
> Some of it was against all form of government, while much of it sought to teach the overthrow of this country's government by force and violence and other unlawful and unconstitutional methods. Several new revolutionary organizations, international in scope, came into existence during the year, and the dissemination of revolutionary {35} propaganda has been systematically conducted, with the result that the would-be revolutionary forces in this country are becoming solidified in thought and action.[31]

The wartime censorship practices of the Department were continued in what was a flagrant attempt by federal officials to stretch the law and thereby meet an alleged emergency.

In one censorship case Burleson initially refused to grant second-class mailing privileges to the *Liberator*, a left-wing monthly, in February, 1918. Each month the magazine applied for a permit. Each month—until the end of the second Wilson administration—permission was refused, although authorities allowed the publication to use the third-class postal facilities. Thus, although the security statutes gave the Postmaster General the power only to exclude disloyal matter, Burleson instead was forcing the *Liberator* to pay a higher mailing rate.[32] This was the situation until Harding's appointment of veteran Republican campaigner Will H. Hays as Burleson's successor. Hays' departmental *Report* for 1921 is a document too little noticed as an affirmation of the value of civil liberties. It is well worth quoting at length here.

"The war is over and it has been the purpose of the department to return to the ordered freedom," Hays

---

[30] *Report of the Postmaster General, 1919,* 112.

[31] *Ibid., 1920,* 125–126.

[32] *Ibid., 1921,* 88–89.

wrote. Reviewing the *Liberator* case, he stated, "The arbitrary power to decide what is and what is not a public benefit was never intended to be lodged in the Postmaster General, and it shall not be assumed by the present management." The Department will not presume to pass judgment on the *Liberator*; it will be admitted to second-class mailing privileges. "There shall be no hesitancy in suppressing any publications that fall within the prohibitions of the public law; but there are also laws in this country safeguarding the integrity of the freedom of the press and these laws must and shall be also scrupulously observed." If the *Liberator* is in fact part of a revolutionary conspiracy, as Burleson has claimed, "then the *Department of Justice* will deal promptly and effectively with the conspirators in the manner prescribed by law."

Hays reaffirmed his faith in the traditional American method {36} of "safeguarding the public welfare while at the same time maintaining freedom of the press," a method which "has been through a long period ... better for the public welfare and personal security of citizens than to establish a bureaucratic censorship which in its nature becomes a matter of individual opinion, prejudice, or caprice."[33]

The President and Mr. Burleson

In May, 1919, the *Nation* published an editorial which undoubtedly did not endear that once-banned magazine to the men in the censor's office. "Surely there never was an official by birth, training, and experience in life so unfit for the task of moulding and controlling public opinion as Albert Sidney Burleson. But in the hue and cry against him, it must not be forgotten that the responsibility for him rests squarely upon Woodrow

---

[33] *Ibid*. Italics added.

Wilson." Wilson had appointed him, the *Nation* asserted, and had tolerated his actions as the country's censor for too long. "Almost every tenet of democracy was violated with scarcely a protest from the great democrat in the White House."[34]

The evidence which is available suggests that the democrat in the White House was aware of some, if not all, of Burleson's excesses. He tried on occasion but with limited success to curb some of Burleson's malpractices; yet in at least one instance he was willing to go even further than the Postmaster General to punish a disloyal published statement. In general, however, Wilson permitted Burleson to have the last word in censorship matters.

This pattern of relationship between the two emerged in the very first days of censorship. On July 17, 1917, Wilson sent a letter to Amos Pinchot, who had protested against the barring from the mails of the New York *Masses*, a Socialist journal; in this letter Wilson forwarded Burleson's justification for barring the issue. Baker asserts that Burleson was "uncompromising in his attitude."[35] Burleson made it clear to the President that he would {37} enforce the Espionage Act and other legislation as he saw fit and that his resignation might follow any attempt at interference.[36]

A few days after writing to Pinchot the President instructed Tumulty to reply to a letter from Oswald Garrison Villard, who also had protested against Burleson's censorship. "He is entirely mistaken about certain papers having been 'suppressed,' " Wilson wrote. "Nothing of the kind occurred. Certain copies of certain newspapers were excluded from the mails because they contained matter

---

[34] Vol. 108 (May 3, 1919), 674.

[35] Baker, *Life and Letters*, VII, 165.

[36] *Ibid.*

explicitly forbidden by law."[37] Thus Wilson recognized the limitations upon the Postmaster General's power prescribed by the Espionage Act. Yet Wilson was intensely concerned over the possible effects of utterances "which would in ordinary circumstances be innocent" but which were liable to be dangerous in wartime.[38] Probably for this reason, he allowed Burleson to stretch his powers to the fullest extent that the courts would allow.

On occasion Wilson did intervene. For example, he persuaded Burleson to reverse a decision to ban the *World Tomorrow* from the mails. One of the persons connected with the paper's management was Nevin Sayre, brother of Wilson's son-in-law. Sayre discussed the suppression with Wilson at a White House dinner on September 13, and three days later the President wrote to Burleson about the matter. On September 19 Sayre informed Wilson that the paper had been admitted to the mails.[39]

Not every publication that Burleson suppressed had the strong friends at court which the *World Tomorrow* could muster. As censorship tightened and the second-class mails were closed to increasing numbers of left-wing publications, Wilson was required to defend Burleson more and more frequently. Three letters were written in October, 1917, in justification of Burleson's actions. On October 18 Wilson wrote to Grenville MacFarland that Burleson was anxious {38} to preserve freedom of the press except when it led to obstruction of the war effort. Four days later Wilson wrote to Herbert

---

[37] *Ibid.*, 178–179. July 20, 1917.

[38] He wrote Max Eastman in September that in time of war "it is legitimate to regard things which would in ordinary circumstances be innocent as very dangerous to the public welfare, but the line is manifestly exceedingly hard to draw" (*ibid.*, 273).

[39] Mock, *Censorship, 1917*, 140; Baker, *Life and Letters*, VIII, 405–406.

Croly of the *New Republic* that Burleson's policies had been misinterpreted and that the Postmaster General was inclined to exercise his vast powers in a moderate fashion. And on the same day the President assured Upton Sinclair that Burleson's censorship policies would prove acceptable when the good intentions of the censor became more obvious.[40]

The President was, it seems, overly sanguine concerning his Postmaster General's intentions. A week before writing the first of these three letters Wilson had sent Burleson an editorial clipped from the Springfield *Republican* which deplored the inroads of censorship upon freedom of the press. With it, the President enclosed a note urging use of "the utmost caution and liberality in all our censorship."[41] The question remained: How much would Wilson himself do to guarantee that his high hopes for fairness in censorship would be realized?[42]

An answer may be found in the Milwaukee *Leader* case. On October 18, 1917, Wilson informed Burleson that he did not approve of the suppression of the *Leader*. "There is a wide margin of judgment here," he stated, "and I think that doubt ought always to be resolved in favor of the utmost freedom of speech." Yet the newspaper, edited by the prominent Socialist Victor Berger, was denied a second-class mailing permit throughout the entire period of Wilson's second administration. Not until May, 1921, was the *Leader*'s permit restored.[43] On occa-

---

[40] Baker *Life and Letters,* VII, 313, 318, 319. Replies to letters which are in File VI, 2244, Wilson Papers.

[41] Note of Oct. 11, 1917, in Baker, *Life and Letters,* VII, 301.

[42] On Oct. 30, 1917, Wilson suggested to Burleson that the newspapers denouncing the war as inspired by Wall Street retain mailing privileges if they allowed equal space for replies by Administration officials. Nothing came of it (letter to Burleson, Wilson Papers).

[43] Hilton, *Southwestern Soc. Sci. Quar.,* XXVIII, 351, 358–359; Baker, *Life and Letters,* VII, 313, quoting Wilson.

sion Wilson's temper got the best of him. For example, he sent a copy of one newspaper to the Attorney General, asking whether it might not provide the basis for indictment of the publisher for treason. Gregory had to inform his {39} chief that the federal criminal code, even as it stood during World War I, did not provide the death penalty for editorial opinions.[44]

The last incident is atypical, however. While the President's attitude was on the whole more lenient than Burleson's, the Postmaster General usually had the last word in censorship matters. Wilson's relations with Burleson are epitomized in the following memorandum on a question concerning newspaper censorship: "I must admit that I haven't been able to read all of the enclosed, but you know that I am willing to trust your judgment after I have once called your attention to a suggestion."[45]

Whether Wilson approved of Burleson' continued censorship in the period following the Armistice is not definitely known. It is certain that Wilson knew of the Postmaster General's refusal to admit to the mails left-wing publications such as the *Liberator*; as late as September, 1920, he suggested to Burleson that censorship policies be discussed by the entire Cabinet.[46] It is obvious that the President did not overrule Burleson if he did disagree with the continued censorship. In his Message of December, 1919, Wilson favored a peacetime sedition statute, and in mid-1920 he killed with a pocket veto the bill that would have terminated the Espionage and Sedition Acts.[47] Thus the President was not totally di-

---

[44] *Ibid.,* 283.

[45] Wilson to Burleson, Sept. 4, 1917, Wilson Papers.

[46] Hilton, *Southwestern Soc. Sci. Quar.,* XXVIII, 355–357.

[47] Swisher, *American Constitutional Development,* 686–687. It should be noted that Burleson ended the censorship over the foreign mails, technically under the jurisdiction of the Board of

vorced in 1918–1921 from that group of government administrators who tended "to regard themselves as wiser and better informed than the people, and under the guise of protecting the people or serving the public welfare to expand their powers in ways never intended by the legislative body."[48]

To explain Wilson's attitude toward the censorship one must consider John Blum's opinion that "the President turned his back on civil liberties not because he loved them less but because he loved his vision of eventual peace much more. To the neglect of other {40} matters, he was preoccupied with the definition and articulation of war aims."[49] Wilson was preoccupied also with the prosecution of the war itself. Furthermore, he was genuinely concerned that seditious utterances might disrupt the war effort. The evidence clearly demonstrates that he preferred to have Burleson go too far rather than chance his not going far enough in stamping out disloyalty. Furthermore, Burleson had proved himself invaluable to the Administration by his handling of patronage,[50] and Wilson was probably unwilling to break with him over any question regarding censorship.[51]

The ultimate tragedy of Burleson's policy was for Wilson himself. George Creel recognized this fact in an explanation of Democratic Congressional losses in 1918:

Censorship, at the time of the Armistice (Burleson to Wilson, Nov. 11, 1918, Wilson Papers).

[48] Hilton, *Southwestern Soc. Sci. Quar.,* XXVIII, 357.

[49] *Woodrow Wilson and the Politics of Morality,* 144.

[50] Link, *Progressive Era,* 29.

[51] Wilson had refused to dismiss Burleson when they differed publicly on a key labor issue: the Postmaster General favored repeal of provisions permitting unionization of government employees in the Lloyd-La Follette Act (Dallas Lee Jones, "The Wilson Administration and Organized Labor, 1912–1919" [Ph.D. dissertation, Cornell University, 1954], 351).

> All the radical or liberal friends of your anti-imperialist war policy were either silenced or intimidated. The Department of Justice and the Post-Office [Department] were allowed to silence or intimidate them. There was no voice left to argue for your sort of peace. When we came to this election the reactionary Republicans had a clean record of anti-Hun imperialistic patriotism. Their opponents, your friends, were often either besmirched or obscure.[52]

The wells of public sentiment were poisoned by intolerant and vindictive nationalism long before the debate on the treaty commenced.[53] Wilson's second administration closed "in a riot of {41} reaction,"[54] and his demand for a peacetime sedition act was merely a part of it. Liberal and progressive support had in many instances been irrevocably lost; Creel's worst fears had in large measure been realized.[55]

---

[52] Quoted in Creel, *The War, the World, and Wilson*, 145–146. An identical view was stated in a memorandum for Colonel House by the National Civil Liberties Bureau, Jan. 24, 1918 (File VI, 3896, Wilson Papers). As a result of suppression of liberal opinion, "discussion of war policies and war aims is now largely in the hands of the 'Tories,'" the Bureau warned.

[53] The word "nationalism" is used here to mean "organic nationalism" as described by Curti, *Roots of American Loyalty*, 179–182. One of the ugliest manifestations of nationalism during the war was the campaign to abolish the teaching and use of the German language. Both repressionists and defenders of German-Americans called upon President Wilson to take a firm stand on this and similar questions. Despite his personal distaste for such repression, Wilson consistently sought to reply without getting himself "involved" (see File VI, 4182, Wilson Papers). Wilson's determination to avoid involvement is most explicitly stated in his note to Tumulty, April 10, 1918, *ibid.*

[54] Richard Hofstadter, *The American Political Tradition* (Vintage ed., New York, 1954), 279.

[55] See Arthur S. Link, "What Happened to the Progressive Movement in the 1920s?" *American Historical Review*, LXIV (1959), 838-839.

IV • The Justice Department

THE Espionage and Sedition Acts were frequently used by the Justice Department, as they were by the Postmaster General, for the punishment and suppression of radicals, pacifists, and other critics of the government's war policies. There were, however, two fundamental differences between the administration of censorship by the Post Office Department and the administration of the security statutes by the Justice Department.

Firstly, the censorship administration was highly centralized, with power vested in an individual official, Burleson, and his immediate subordinates.[1] In the Justice Department control over federal district attorneys throughout the nation was held to a minimum until a few weeks before the Armistice.

Secondly, the intentions of the highest officers in the Justice Department were vastly different from those of Burleson. In contrast with Burleson's administrative directives was Attorney General Gregory's opinion that the Justice Department "is not only responsible for law enforcement, but, in a larger sense, is responsible for the protection of civil liberty."[2] John Lord O'Brian and Alfred Bettman, who shared in the administration of the security statutes, were {43} in full agreement with this maxim.[3]

---

[1] Mail leaving the United States was censored by a large staff, but banning from the domestic mails, denial of second-class mailing permits, and decisions to refuse to deliver mail were all handled in Burleson's office.

[2] *Report of the Attorney General, 1918,* 16.

[3] Chafee, *Free Speech,* 67. It must be recalled that Gregory, as did all the Cabinet members, tolerated the policy of discrimination

Yet throughout the war years these high officials failed to impress their own generally tolerant attitudes upon their subordinates in the field. The decentralization which characterized the administration of the Department of Justice resulted in many prosecutions based on standards of neither fair play nor common sense. There was wide variation from district to district in the application of the laws, as many district attorneys succumbed to their own prejudices or to local pressure.[4] Furthermore, the Department unwisely delegated many functions to the American Protective League, an officially recognized auxiliary with 250,000 members under the control of the district attorneys. Often exceeding or ignoring orders, these amateur detectives indulged in illegal arrests and searches, impersonation of federal officers, and irresponsible propaganda activities. By the time of the Armistice it had become obvious that the League was a stronghold of reactionary elements. A source of embarrassment to the Administration, the organization lost its official status shortly thereafter.[5]

The federal judiciary—termed "hysterical" by Justice Oliver Wendell Holmes—proved to be highly immoderate in passing on Espionage and Sedition Act cases.[6] Jurymen were reported by one judge to have regarded verdicts of guilty as a means of demonstrating their own

---

against Negroes in the civil service. See K. L. Wolgemuth, "Woodrow Wilson and Federal Segregation," *Journal of Negro History,* XLIV (1959), 158–173.

[4] O'Brian, *Harvard Law Review, LXVI*, 12.

[5] Robert K. Murray, *Red Scare: A Study in National Hysteria, 1919-1920* (Minneapolis, 1955), 12; A. Mitchell Palmer to Tumulty, March 15, 1920, File VI, 20, Wilson Papers. Harold M. Hyman, *To Try Men's Souls: Loyalty Tests in American History* (Berkeley, 1959), 271–297, is a full study of the A.P.L.

[6] Holmes to Harold Laski, March 16, 1919, in Mark DeW. Howe, ed., *Holmes-Laski Letters* (Cambridge, 1953), 190.

loyalty.[7] Under these conditions it was essential that {44} some manner of firm control be exercised in order to ensure that civil liberties would be respected by federal agents. Despite generally good intentions on the part of the highest officers in the Justice Department, a distinct administrative failure was the cause of many deplorable abuses.

Good Intentions

Although Gregory asserted that "the constitutional right of free speech, free assembly, and petition exist in war time as in peace time," the line between harmless criticism and remarks dangerous to the war effort was manifestly difficult to draw.[8] As we have seen, Gregory's fear of "casual or impulsive disloyal utterances" led him to demand a sedition act in early 1918. Occasionally this fear led him to make ill-considered public statements, as when he warned "those disloyal persons and moral and physical degenerates who believe nothing worth fighting for" to expect no mercy from "an avenging Government."[9] His distrust of dissident elements also led him, in the winter of 1917–1918, to turn that avenging government in all its full fury upon the International Workers of the World, thus crippling the movement; and it prompted his decision to indict Eugene Debs in 1918.[10]

---

[7] Mock, *Censorship, 1917*, 198. Upon reviewing Espionage Act judicial decisions after the Armistice, Justice Department officials found that many judges imposed severe sentences as a means of fostering unity and bolstering morale (stenographic report of a statement by A. M. Palmer to Samuel Gompers and others, Sept. 14, 1920, File VI, 3896, Wilson Papers, and letter from a federal judge to Gregory, Aug. 12, 1918, Gregory Papers).

[8] *Report of the Attorney General, 1918*, 20.

[9] Quoted in New York *Times*, Nov. 21, 1917.

[10] See Ray Ginger, *The Bending Cross: A Biography of Eugene Victor Debs* (New Brunswick, 1949), 330 ff.; Murray, *Red Scare*, 21–25, 30–31; Peterson and Fite, *Opponents of War, passim;* and,

The Attorney General's intentions were revealed in several letters of instruction to the district attorneys, both before and during the war. Upon receipt of the German submarine note of January 31, 1917, it became evident that war might ensue, and Gregory prepared to intern known German agents and to protect military and naval installations from sabotage.[11] In a directive of March 27 he warned his subordinates to avoid making "unwarranted arrests or to cause apprehension on the part of [the foreign] population," and he ordered federal attorneys to "arrange that all contemplated arrests, in so far as circumstances permit, be submitted to the department {45} for consideration."[12] Upon American entry into the war Gregory drafted for the President the Proclamation of April 6 which authorized internment of enemy aliens. Once again Gregory directed federal attorneys to receive authorization from Washington before making arrests.[13] Some critics have condemned the philosophy of arbitrary internment.[14] It is, however, significant that in this single area of action in which high Justice Department officials maintained close control over their subordinates abuses were apparently held to a minimum. Of approximately 3,500,000 enemy aliens believed to have been in the United States during the war, 6,300 were arrested and of these 2,300 actually interned.[15] Caution and forbearance

---

for Gregory's attitude toward the Irish-Americans, many of whom he believed to be disloyal, Gregory to Colonel House, June 10, 1920, Gregory Papers.

[11] O'Brian, *Harvard Law Review,* LXVI, 9.

[12] *Report of the Attorney General, 1917,* 55.

[13] *Ibid.,* 62–63.

[14] See Peterson and Fite, *Opponents of War,* 86 and 86 n. 16.

[15] See *Report of the Attorney General, 1918,* 26. When the University of Texas in April, 1917, dismissed all aliens on the staff, Gregory permitted his friends to distribute the following statement by him: "The Administration is firmly convinced that one of the grave dangers confronting this nation is that our own people will not be

characterized the centralized administration of the alien-enemy proclamations.

Had the Attorney General acted in a similar fashion to centralize Espionage and Sedition Act enforcement, a national disgrace might well have been avoided. Instead, Gregory permitted district attorneys to enjoy their customary freedom in prosecuting cases, merely warning them that "care should be exercised to avoid unjustified arrests and prosecution."[16] When many attorneys proved irresponsible, Gregory appointed several special assistants, responsible directly to himself, to take over the war functions of his "unmanageable" subordinates.[17] Finally, having become aware of an "increasing conflict of opinion in interpreting the law," Gregory was {46} forced to take drastic action.[18] On the advice of the President he ordered federal attorneys to receive approval from Washington before presenting security cases to grand juries. This order went into effect on October 28, 1918, and although prosecutions continued after the Armistice the number of presentments declined.[19] By June 30, 1919,

---

sufficiently liberal in their treatment of aliens. . . . Any improper or unreasonable attack upon this class of people could only produce trouble" (letter to D. W. Jones, April 28, 1917, Gregory Papers).

[16] Quoted in *Official Bulletin,* May 27, 1918. Cases under the treason statutes were required to be prosecuted with prior approval of the Attorney General, but there were few prosecutions, none of them successful (*Report of the Attorney General, 1918,* 21).

[17] O'Brian, *Harvard Law Review,* LXVI, 12.

[18] *Report of the Attorney General, 1918,* 22. Gregory had earlier expressed his views on the problem of centralization as follows: "I am dealing with a large number of men of varying ability and character, many of them in very remote sections of the country, and. . . I am practically charged with all the mistakes any of them make. . . .I feel [however] that the views of the local district attorney. . . should be acquiesced in except in most unusual cases" (letter to G. W. Anderson, May 16, 1916, Gregory Papers).

[19] Baker, *Life and Letters,* VIII, 460; *Report of the Attorney General, 1918,* 22.

more than four hundred cases already brought to court had been discontinued.[20]

Before leaving office in March, 1919, Gregory reviewed the court proceedings which had resulted in Espionage Act convictions during the war. As a result he recommended to the President more than one hundred commutations of sentence for convicted persons still in prison, on the grounds that "injustice [had] resulted to certain defendants because of the all-prevalent conditions of intense patriotism and aroused emotion on the part of the jurors." Gregory further asserted that in certain cases the sentences had been out of all proportion to the offense.[21] Had the Attorney General acted earlier to quash the ruthlessness of some of his subordinates, many outrages might have been averted.

The Fruits of Decentralization

A tabulation of prosecutions under the Espionage and Sedition Acts, 1917 to 1921, reveals striking district-to-district variations in the number of persons indicted.[22] A total of 2,168 were brought to trial, forty-six of them after June 30, 1919. Of these, 2,036 trials {47} were terminated by June 30, 1921, of which 1,055 were convictions, 181 acquittals, 665 discontinued, and 135 quashed or dismissed.

Some of the irresponsible district attorneys were doubtless operating in the districts which reported fifty or

---

[20] See Appendix.

[21] Gregory to Wilson, March 1, 1919, Wilson Papers; New York *Times,* April 12, March 3, 1919. As of Sept. 14, 1920, there remained 174 persons in prison for violation of security statutes (stenographic report of statement by A. M. Palmer, Sept. 14, 1920, Wilson Papers).

[22] This tabulation appears in the Appendix.

more prosecutions.²³ These included Arizona (99 cases); Northern District, California (78); Southern, California (57); Southern, Illinois (67); Eastern, Kentucky (56); Eastern, Missouri (103); Southern, New York (55); North Dakota (103); Southern, Texas (82); Western, Texas (89); Western, State of Washington (54); Western, Wisconsin (62); and Northern, Illinois (141).²⁴ *Thus the prosecutions in only thirteen of the eighty-seven federal districts accounted for almost one-half of the total number of prosecutions under the Espionage and Sedition Acts; that is, 1,046 out of 2,168 prosecutions.*

Some of the best-known cases of overzealous prosecution took place in these districts. For example, the federal attorney in North Dakota prosecuted the case against Kate Richards O'Hare, who was sentenced to five years' imprisonment for a speech which she had previously delivered without hindrance in several cities outside North Dakota.²⁵ The federal attorney in the Eastern District, Missouri, pressed a case against a man accused of saying, "To hell with Wilson; I am a Republican." Fortunately the presiding judge dismissed the case.²⁶ The notorious "slacker raid" of September, 1918, in the Southern District of New York was marked by brutal and illegal methods. American Protective League volunteers, soldiers and sailors, and Justice Department agents summarily arrested 20,000 men, dragging many from street-

---

[23] Only Southern District, New York, and Northern District, Illinois—of the districts listed—contained exceptionally large populations. Most of the others listed are of average district population or less.

[24] The figure for Northern Illinois includes I.W.W. prosecutions, listed under Draft Act cases in *Report of the Attorney General, 1918,* 179.

[25] N.C.L.B., "The Conviction of Mrs. Kate Richards O'Hare" (pamphlet, New York, 1918), 10–11. Yet Gregory may have approved in this case because of its unusual importance.

[26] Peterson and Fite, *Opponents of War,* 141.

cars and offices. Gregory reported to Wilson that the Department officials in New York had {48} acted against the specific instructions of the Attorney General.[27] When in the same month Justice Department agents sacked the offices of the National Civil Liberties Bureau, it was again without the permission of the Attorney General.[28]

In 1919 the Department of Justice reviewed all Espionage Act convictions of persons still in prison. Commutations were granted to 116 prisoners whose convictions were deemed unfair or sentences overly long. The district court which convicted is known for 108 of these cases; and of the 108, forty-three persons were convicted in the thirteen districts listed above.[29]

It should also be noted that almost all the districts reporting high incidences of prosecutions were areas in which the I.W.W. was active.[30] In these localities federal officers were under pressure from employers and patriotic societies, who charged the union with disloyalty and used violence against "Wobbly" workers and leaders.[31] By September, 1917, the Wilson Cabinet had determined to crush the I.W.W., using both the Army and the Justice

---

[27] Letter to Wilson, Sept. 9, 1918, Gregory Papers.

[28] Nelles, *A Liberal in Wartime,* 151–152.

[29] The total number of district courts whose convictions were affected was forty-five (compiled from "Warrants signed by the President, April 22, 1919," in File VI, 20, Wilson Papers; "Warrants signed March 2, 1919," in File VI, 3896, *ibid.;* and Palmer to Wilson, May 9, 10, 15, 1919, *ibid.*).

[30] The union was especially active among migrant workers in the Dakota wheat fields, the iron ranges of Michigan and Minnesota, and in California, Arizona, Washington, Idaho, Montana, and Colorado.

[31] Paul F. Brissenden, *The I.W.W.: A Study of American Syndicalism* (New York, 1920), 10; N.C.L.B., "War-time Prosecutions and Mob Violence," *passim;* N.C.L.B., "The Truth about the I.W.W." (pamphlet, Washington, 1918), 20 ff.

Department in its attack.³² The prominence of Bill Haywood and other I.W.W. leaders among the opponents of the war, the pressure from reactionary local patriotic organizations, and fear of further vigilante violence probably combined to produce the Cabinet decision.

Thus, while decentralization explains the large number of prosecutions under the Espionage and Sedition Acts in many of the {49} federal districts, the Administration campaign against the I.W.W. was also a factor.

The President and the Attorney General

President Wilson permitted Gregory to work out his own administrative problems, intervening rarely in Justice Department affairs.³³ Statements which Wilson made privately confirm the impression that he placed confidence in Gregory's ability.³⁴ Several wartime incidents will serve to illustrate their relationship:

1. In June, 1917, Wilson expressed to Gregory his disapproval of the American Protective League. "It seems to me it would be very dangerous to have such an organization operating in the United States," he wrote.³⁵ Gregory, however, insisted that the auxiliary force was needed by the Justice Department, and Wilson yielded. When League members were reported acting as agents provocateurs, or posing as federal officers (in at least one case annoying a United States Senator), Gregory kept up a

---

³² Preston, "Ideology and Techniques," 249; Edward S. Corwin, *The President: Office and Powers* (New York, 1948), 166; Bennet M. Rich, *The Presidents and Civil Disorder* (Washington, 1941), 156. The "war" on the I.W.W. is described ably in Peterson and Fite, *Opponents of War, passim*.

³³ Gregory to Josephus Daniels, Feb. 19, 1924, Gregory Papers.

³⁴ Cummings and MacFarland, *Federal Justice,* 423.

³⁵ Quoted in Peterson and Fite, *Opponents of War,* 19.

bold front.[36] "This country was never so thoroughly policed in its history," he boasted.[37] Upon announcement of the Armistice in November, 1918, the Attorney General ordered the League to deposit in Washington its records of "complaints, rumors, and investigations."[38] In February the organization was ordered to disband. Had Gregory accepted Wilson's advice of June, 1917, many injustices might have been avoided. Had the President insisted that Gregory accept his advice, the same end would have been served.

2. A second instance in which Wilson concerned himself with Justice Department affairs found him in agreement with Gregory. In April, 1918, Assistant Attorney General Charles Warren, who had previously been responsible for drafting security measures, proposed a "court martial bill" to the Senate Military Affairs Committee. Under its terms persons interfering with the war effort {50} would have been tried by military courts and subject to the death penalty.[39] Gregory immediately denounced the proposals as "subversive of fundamental principles of justice," and President Wilson concurred. Wilson informed the Senate that he was "wholly and inalterably opposed to such legislation."[40] Although it is doubtful that the bill received much support in the Senate, the President's outspoken opposition ended the affair in short order.[41]

---

[36] The Senator was George Norris (Norris, *Fighting Liberal* [New York, 1945], 199–201).

[37] *Official Bulletin*, April 19, 1918.

[38] O'Brian, *Harvard Law Review*, LXVI, 13.

[39] New York *Times*, April 20, 1918.

[40] Gregory is quoted in Cummings and MacFarland, *Federal Justice*, 424; Wilson, in Baker, *Life and Letters*, VIII, 100–101.

[41] New York *Times*, April 17, 23, 1918.

3. In the spring of 1918 patriotic societies, local Councils of National Defense, and mobs condemned and attacked pacifists, German-Americans, Socialists, and other alleged traitors in what amounted to a wave of terror.[42] President Wilson was aware of the upsurge of intolerance and hysteria. In April and May, 1918, he wrote at least five letters expressing sympathy for German-Americans who were the victims of persecution. "I have a very great passion for the principle that we must respect opinion even when it is hostile," he wrote.[43] Unfortunately his "passion" did not impel him to take prompt measures to end the series of excesses. Americans aware of the government's attack upon the I.W.W. and of Burleson's campaign against the left-wing press must have concluded that the danger from within was still great. Despite innumerable requests from private citizens and public officials that he condemn mob violence in a strong, well-publicized statement, Wilson deemed it best not to involve himself.[44]

By April 4 many citizens were prepared to bring mob justice to "traitors" who kept within the law.[45] Five hundred such citizens in {51} Collinsville, Illinois, who had decided that a fellow townsman, Robert Prager, was a German spy, dragged him into the street, wrapped him in the flag, and then murdered him. "There is quite a deal of hysteria in the country about German spies," Gregory

---

[42] See Peterson and Fite, *Opponents of War,* 194 ff.

[43] Baker, *Life and Letters,* VIII, 102–103, and *passim.*

[44] See petitions and correspondence in Files VI, 20, 543, 3896, 4138, and 4182, Wilson Papers. Much of the pressure upon Wilson to condemn mob violence publicly came from Negro leaders, for more than 250 Negroes were lynched during the war years (*Journal of Negro Education,* XII [1943], Yearbook Issue; and Jane L. Scheiber and H. N. Scheiber, "The Wilson Administration and the Mobilization of Black Americans," *Labor History,* 10 (1969), 433-58.

[45] See Wilson's address of June 14, 1917, *Congress. Rec.,* LV, Appendix, 334.

wrote. "The reasons for the lynching of the man in Illinois, and of others throughout the country, are being set forth in constantly reiterated statements which are absolutely without foundation."[46] Although many of Wilson's subordinates were alarmed and made public statements condemning vigilante justice, the President himself delayed doing so until July 26. The four-month delay is difficult to explain.[47]

4. On October 7, 1918, Wilson wrote to Gregory, enclosing a letter from a correspondent who complained that the Attorney General's office upheld the actions of federal attorneys whatever their course. Wilson asserted that reactionary groups in many localities were employing the security statutes for their own purposes: "As a matter of fact, we are in danger of playing into the hands of some violently and maliciously partisan Republicans." He concluded his memorandum with a comment which went to the root of the Justice Department problem: "It might have a fine effect if this whole business could be put upon the basis you and I would put it upon if we were handling it ourselves."[48] It is tragic that this was not accomplished until the month before the Armistice, when Gregory finally centralized administration of the Espionage and Sedition Acts.

---

[46] Letter to T. U. Taylor, April 15, 1918, Gregory Papers.

[47] Among federal officials who made public statements after the Prager lynching were Gregory and Arthur H. Fleming (Chief of the State Councils Section, Council of National Defense). Others who urged that a public denunciation of lynching be made included Secretary Newton Baker and John Lord O'Brian (*Crisis,* XVI [June, 1918], 71; Fleming to Wilson with enclosures, July 24, 1918, Wilson Papers; Baker to Wilson, July 1, 1918, *ibid.;* O'Brian, "Memorandum for the Attorney General, April 18, 1918," *ibid.*).

[48] Baker, *Life and Letters,* VIII, 460.

V • The Red Scare

WHILE THERE may have been some justification for the harsh repression of dissident groups during the war, there was none for the excesses in which the government indulged during the Red Scare of 1919–1920. High officials in the government, notably Attorney General A. Mitchell Palmer, deliberately fanned the flames of fear and prejudice. In June, 1919, Palmer (who succeeded Gregory in March, 1919) opened a broad campaign against an alleged revolutionary menace. Summary arrests, brutal interrogations, and arbitrary mass deportations characterized federal action during the Red Scare.[1]

The history of the antiradical campaign is usually written without reference to the role of the President. Many students of the Red Scare accept the judgment of Frederick Lewis Allen that "Woodrow Wilson was ill in the White House, out of touch with affairs, and dreaming only of his lamented League: That is the only explanation."[2] In fact, the President should not be absolved of all {53} responsibility. He appointed Palmer and tolerated his actions. Before his paralytic stroke in October, 1919, Wilson made several public pronouncements—particu-

---

[1] See Murray, *Red Scare;* Robert D. Warth, "The Palmer Raids," *South Atlantic Quarterly,* XLVIII (1949), 1–23; Preston W. Slosson, *The Great Crusade and After, 1914–1928* (New York, 1930), 79 ff.; Frederic L. Paxson, *American Democracy and the World War,* vol. III, "Postwar Years" (Berkeley, 1948), *passim;* Peterson and Fite, *Opponents of War,* 285–296. Murray's is the fullest treatment.

[2] *Only Yesterday: An Informal History of the 1920's* (Bantam ed., New York, 1952), 49. See Chafee, *Free Speech,* 214; Murray, *Red Scare,* 11, 200.

larly during his League tour—which played on the public mood of fear and prejudice, and in December Wilson asked Congress to pass a peacetime sedition act. The impression that revolutionary elements were an actual danger in the United States was further dignified by Wilson's refusal, until the closing days of his administration, to sign Congressional bills which would have terminated the Espionage and Sedition Acts. These actions and utterances are by no means irrelevant to the history of the Red Scare.

Wilson's Conception of Reconstruction

In June, 1918, Wilson confided to his brother-in-law that he believed the postwar world would require broad government intervention in economic affairs. He is reported to have said, "I am satisfied for instance that the government will have to take over . . . all the water power, all the coal mines, all the oil fields." He would be called a socialist because of these ideas and could not express them publicly, he said, yet this program was for him the only practical alternative to communism.[3]

By the war's end, however, Wilson's mind had changed.[4] He stated before Congress in December, 1918, that there were no comprehensive economic programs which both business and labor would accept and that government would merely "mediate the process of change."[5] Yet the President was more fearful than ever of the dangers from revolution in the world.[6] He believed that the United States had a "tremendous responsibility

---

[3] Quoted in Baker, *Life and Letters*, VIII, 241–242. It is ironic that on the same day Eugene Debs was arrested in Cleveland for interfering with recruitment because his condemnation of the capitalist class discouraged enlistments.

[4] See Hofstadter, *The American Political Tradition*, 278.

[5] Speech of Dec. 12, 1918, *Public Papers*, V, 313.

[6] See Baker, *Life and Letters*, VIII, 553.

... to see that the world did not fall into chaos"[7] and devoted himself in the first six months of 1919 almost entirely to the Peace Conference in Paris. {54} During that time, domestic problems multiplied, and the direction of the federal government was left largely to others.[8]

Events at Home, 1919

Widespread labor unrest immediately following the Armistice set off a renewed antilabor, antiradical campaign.[9] Employers attempted to identify the unions with the dreaded radicalism. To persuade the public that a strike was instigated by Bolshevist agents was to win public sympathy, and such arguments contributed to the heightening national fear of foreign isms. Furthermore, repressionist groups attempted to identify the radical with the alien, and with a large measure of success, for many foreign-born were active in the left-wing movements. The fact that the American public tolerated some of the lawless features of the Palmer Raids at the end of 1919 is evidence that the campaign of hate had enjoyed considerable success.

Mounting pressure for the state governments to act against the radical menace resulted, and by 1920 thirty-six states had passed statutes outlawing seditious utterances or display of the red flag.[10] On March 28, 1919,

---

[7] *Ibid.*, 581.

[8] Message to Congress, May 20, 1919, *Public Papers*, V, 486.

[9] See George Soule, *Prosperity Decade* (New York, 1947), 81 ff., and the works cited in note 1 of this chapter. Negro leaders bitterly refuted the widely repeated assertion that race riots were the result of Bolshevist activity rather than of tensions arising from maltreatment of Negroes (J. E. Bruce to Editor, N.Y. *Herald* [1919], Bruce Papers, New York Public Library; Handy L. Duncan to Wilson, Aug. 4, 1919, Wilson Papers).

[10] Link, *American Epoch*, 242; Handlin, *American People in 20th Century*, 146.

Attorney General Palmer announced that he would request of Congress a peacetime sedition act; in June, Palmer testified before a Congressional committee that he had been advised of the date of an impending revolution.[11] No contradiction of Palmer's remarkable contention was forthcoming from the White House. In fact, in the months prior to his illness President Wilson contributed to that mood of fear and intolerance which was the ultimate source of Palmer's power. {55}

The League Tour

On September 4, 1919, Wilson embarked on a speaking tour in which he carried the issue of the Treaty of Paris to the electorate. The tour was of great moment, and it is important to examine Wilson's speeches to determine Wilson's views on two subjects then dominant in the public mind: the alien and the radical.[12]

Wilson's major argument for the League was that it would be an effective means for preventing future war. He appealed to American altruism and to the need for this nation to assume world leadership to avert future conflict. A second argument for immediate acceptance of the treaty and the League was concerned with the possibility of revolution in Europe and in the United States. If Europeans were not assured of a new international order, Wilson asserted, they would destroy their governments.[13]

---

[11] New York *Times,* March 29, 1919; Labor Research Association, *The Palmer Raids,* ed. Robert W. Dunn (New York, 1948), 49.

[12] For accounts of the tour, see Dexter Perkins, "Woodrow Wilson's Tour" in *America in Crisis,* ed. Daniel Aaron (New York, 1952), 245–266; Denna Frank Fleming, *The United States and the League of Nations, 1918 – 1920* (New York, 1932), 347–358; Thomas A. Bailey, *Woodrow Wilson and the Great Betrayal* (New York, 1945), 90–122; and C. R. Henderlider, "Woodrow Wilson's Speeches on the League of Nations," *Speech Monographs,* XIII (1946), 23–34.

[13] *Public Papers,* VI, 69–70, 100–101.

He argued further that America was not immune; that "the poison of disorder, the poison of revolt, the poison of chaos," all had worked their way "into the veins of this free people."[14] He warned his audiences as follows:

> Just so certainly as [Europeans] are disconcerted, thrown back upon their own resources, disheartened, rendered cynical by the withdrawal of the only people in the world they trust, just so certainly there will be universal upsetting of order in Europe. And if the order of Europe is upset, do you think America is going to be quiet? Have you not been reading in the papers of the intolerable thing that has just happened in Boston? When the police of a great city walk out and leave that city to be looted they have committed an intolerable crime against civilization.[15] {56}

Wilson thus linked a strike by an underpaid staff of city police with world revolution.

The President did not advocate lawless or violent methods of dealing with radicals; in fact, he counseled specifically against such means.[16] Yet his assertions concerning the menace of revolution to American institutions were not designed to allay the passions and fears of a concerned people. Nor was his attitude toward the foreign-born a tolerant one. In the campaign of 1916 and during the neutrality period, as we have seen, Wilson had frequently attacked his foreign-born opponents as disloyal to the United States. This theme emerged once again in his defense of his treaty: "There is an organized propaganda against the League of Nations and against the treaty proceeding from exactly the same sources ... which threatened this country here and there with disloy-

---

[14] "Addresses of President Wilson, September 4-September 15, 1919," 66th Cong., 1st Sess., Sen. Doc. 120 (Washington, 1919), 60. See Barbara K. Shelton, "President Wilson and the Russian Revolution," in *University of Buffalo Studies,* XXIII (1957), 151–152.

[15] "Addresses of President Wilson," 159.

[16] *Public Papers,* VI, 111, 136.

alty.... Any man who carries a hyphen about with him carries a dagger that he is ready to plunge into the vitals of this Republic."[17]

Many foreign-born Americans were in fact dissatisfied with the treaty, especially with its failure to fulfill the nationalistic aspirations of European minorities.[18] Yet to term the opposition to the treaty disloyal was to go far beyond the bounds of reason. Since 1916 the foreign-born and left-wing elements in American politics had felt the effects of Wilson's appeals to superpatriotism and prejudice, and now these groups were firmly aligned against the President. In 1919 Woodrow Wilson tasted the bitter fruits of the long years of divisiveness and repression. Only this can explain his pathetic efforts to use such time-worn phrases and distorted arguments in his League tour.

The Last Months

It is impossible to hold Wilson fully accountable for the policies of his administration during the notorious Palmer Raids of January, 1920, or the remainder of his term of office.[19] Devastating illness {57} had made of this proud fighter an embittered, crippled old man. As a result, "strong men in the Cabinet ran their own departments and plotted to win the succession."[20] Palmer and Burleson were purposeful men, and they were among those who wielded a free hand. Actually, Burleson did not enjoy a great deal less freedom in administering censor-

---

[17] "Addresses of President Wilson," 359–360.

[18] Selig Adler, *The Isolationist Impulse: Its Twentieth Century Reaction* (New York, 1957), 80 ff.; Perkins, "Woodrow Wilson's Tour," 254.

[19] For the Palmer Raids, see Louis F. Post, *The Deportations Delirium of 1920* (Chicago, 1923) and the works cited in note 1 of this chapter.

[20] John A. Garraty, *Woodrow Wilson* (New York, 1956), 188.

ship after the Armistice than he had during the war itself. As for Wilson's relationship with Palmer, the League tour speeches demonstrate that the President shared Palmer's fear of Bolshevism. The portion of Wilson's December, 1919, Message to Congress in which he recommended passage of a sedition bill is strikingly similar to other pronouncements that he had made on the subject prior to his illness.[21] During the last months of his term of office Wilson refused to sign a bill which would have terminated some of the security measures under which Cabinet officers were suppressing fundamental American liberties. Until the day before he left office, Wilson refused to surrender wartime powers.[22] A general amnesty to persons convicted under the security statutes would have helped to allay the postwar hysteria. Yet Eugene Debs and others remained behind bars because the President's advisers, while admitting that many sentences were either unjust or too severe, found it inexpedient to pardon all the convicted.[23] These actions alienated important liberal groups, serving to disrupt further the progressive coalition that had been the basis of Wilson's power in earlier years. The Democratic party would have

---

[21] *Public Papers,* VI, 111, 434.

[22] Both Elihu Root and (after resigning from office) and John Lord O'Brian denounced continued operation of wartime statutes (Robert Bacon and James B. Scott, eds., *Men and Policies: Addresses by Elihu Root* [Cambridge, 1924], 206; New York *Times,* Feb. 21, 1920).

[23] There is evidence that in November, 1918, Wilson would probably have granted a general amnesty to Espionage Act offenders but was dissuaded by his Attorney General (Wilson to Gregory, Nov. 20, 1918, and reply, Nov. 29, 1913, Gregory Papers). Both Gregory and Palmer recognized the fact that injustices had been done and recommended commutations of sentences; but neither approved of a general amnesty. Debs, however, was clearly the victim of a political decision (Peterson and Fite, *Opponents of War,* 270–271; and stenographic report of a statement by Palmer to Samuel Gompers and others, Sept. 14, 1920, Wilson Papers).

{58} to pay the price for this legacy of bitterness. When Carl Becker visited Wilson in the house on S Street shortly after Harding's inauguration, Wilson seemed to Becker to be desperately holding on to the belief that he had not entirely failed.[24] Wilson could have derived little solace from his record in the field of civil liberties.

Damage to many lives had been done, and it was often irreparable.[25] The nation too had lost, for the years of victorious war abroad were sad years at home. Some curtailment of liberties is to be expected in wartime, yet as Professor Robert Cushman has stated, "the record of our behavior with respect to civil liberties during World War I is not one in which the thoughtful citizen can take much pride or satisfaction."[26]

---

[24] Becker to Frederick Lewis Allen, March 19, 1933, Carl Becker Papers, Regional History Collection, Cornell University Library.

[25] For the protests of Clarence Darrow, Upton Sinclair, Norman Hapgood, Samuel Gompers, and others against the continued imprisonment in 1919–1920 of Espionage Act offenders, see File VI, 4963, Wilson Papers. The last of these prisoners was released in 1923, when the United States Pardon Attorney concluded that there was "very little evidence that many of these defendants ever did anything to constitute a violation of the Espionage Act" (quoted in Preston, "Ideology and Techniques," 258). Justice Holmes had written earlier of Espionage Act convictions that "those whose cases have come before us have seemed to me poor fools whom I should have been inclined to pass over if I could" (M. DeW. Howe, ed., *Holmes-Pollack Letters* [Cambridge, 1951], II, 11).

[26] "Civil Liberty after the War," *American Political Science Review*, XXXVIII (1944), 6.

Conclusion

THE YEARS 1917–1921 marked an unprecedented sacrifice of civil liberty in the United States. Aware that repressive measures might have ugly consequences, President Wilson nevertheless requested and obtained legislation designed to punish "seditious" utterances and writings in an effort to tighten the system of internal security. This legislation vested the President and his Cabinet with wide discretionary powers. In the Justice Department subordinate officers exercised considerable autonomy, frequently unwisely; in the Post Office Department the Postmaster General personally employed his censorship power to suppress the weak, generally left-wing "subsidiary press." The menace to traditional liberties was intensified by the actions of private citizens, for mob action against those accused of disloyalty was a significant element in the national scene throughout the war years. The nativist and antiradical prejudices which often actuated exponents of vigilante justice—and those who tolerated such repression—had been manifest before 1917, and involvement in total war provided a convenient excuse for imposing total conformity. Denunciations of alleged disloyalty among aliens and radicals broadened into a wide campaign to impose a conservative, antiforeign, nationalist ideology. And the arguments of repressionist groups were dignified by the broadly publicized federal campaign against Socialists, pacifists, the I.W.W., and critics of intervention popularly associated with the foreign-born. Furthermore, these arguments {60} appealed strongly to those who simply feared the effects of disunity in wartime.

To what extent could President Wilson have moderated the passions of war? Wilson was constantly at the center of the public stage during his Presidency, as domestic reformer, architect of American neutrality, commander-in-chief, and, finally, formulator of American war aims. No President, however dynamic and forceful, could have ruled public sentiment, yet Wilson certainly could have influenced it significantly. He was called upon repeatedly to state his personal views on the subject of repression, but he never demonstrated a willingness to exercise vigilance in the cause of freedom of speech and press. Rather, he generally avoided taking a strong public stand on these questions, even when he privately disapproved of particular repressions. Indeed, from 1916 through the war years he was frequently harshly critical of the groups accused of disloyalty when he referred to them in his public addresses.

It was the first occasion since the Civil War that curtailment of basic liberties had become a substantial national question, and executive responsibility was urgently needed. Beset by the problems attendant to expanded wartime government, Wilson sought to avoid what he considered unnecessary involvement in the administration of security legislation. The results varied according to the individual to whom he delegated power. His abdication of personal responsibility left the fate of civil liberties to subordinate officials, the judiciary, and the public at a time when few were inclined to be moderate and when regard for freedom of speech and press appeared to be the particular concern of unpopular dissident minorities.

APPENDIX

Criminal Prosecution under the Espionage Act[1]

		Commenced during the fiscal year ended 30 June:			
District Court	*Population*[2]	1918	1919	1920	1921
Northern, Alabama	1,037,123	10	9	--	--
Middle, Alabama	684,298	2	2	--	--
Southern, Alabama	416,672	1	1	--	--
Alaska, 1st Division	64,356	5	3	--	--
Alaska, 2nd Division	64,356	1	--	--	--
Alaska, 3rd Division	64,356	3	2	--	--
Alaska, 4th Division	64,356	--	--	--	--
Arizona	204,354	47	46	6	--
Eastern, Arkansas	986,380	4	--	--	--
Western, Arkansas	588,069	8	2	--	--
Northern, California	1,407,368	25	52	1	--
Southern, California	907,181	18	39	--	--

---

[1] Compiled from the *Reports* of the Attorney General, 1918–1921. The term "Espionage Act" includes the act of June 15, 1917, and the so-called "Sedition Act," or amendments of May 16, 1918.

[2] According to the 1910 census.

74 • THE WILSON ADMINISTRATION AND CIVIL LIBERTIES

District Court	Population	Commenced during the fiscal year ended 30 June:			
		1918	1919	1920	1921
Colorado	799,024	13	--	--	--
Connecticut	1,114,756	7	19	--	--
Delaware	202,322	1	--	1	--
District of Columbia	331,069	--	4	1	--
Northern, Florida	266,649	12	3	--	--
Southern, Florida	485,970	1	13	3	--
Northern, Georgia	1,254,328	5	12	--	--
Southern, Georgia	1,354,793	1	1	--	--
Hawaii	191,909	2	1	--	--
Idaho	325,594	16	16	--	--
Northern, Illinois[3]	3,107,261	7	18	--	3
Eastern, Illinois	1,195,361	6	6	--	--
Southern, Illinois	1,335,969	33	33	1	--
Indiana	2,700,876	16	3	--	1
Northern, Iowa	1,058,101	10	1	--	--
Southern, Iowa	1,166,949	13	2	2	--
Kansas[3]	1,690,949	8	2	--	--
Eastern, Kentucky	1,118,343	11	45	--	--
Western, Kentucky	1,171,562	4	7	--	--
Eastern, Louisiana	827,478	7	5	1	--
Western, Louisiana	828,910	9	3	--	--
Maine	742,371	--	--	--	--
Maryland	1,295,346	1	2	--	--
Massachusetts	3,366,416	5	--	--	--

[3] See explanatory note above "Total Prosecutions" near end of table.

		Commenced during the fiscal year ended 30 June:			
District Court	*Population*	*1918*	*1919*	*1920*	*1921*
Eastern, Michigan	1,621,270	5	17	--	--
Western, Michigan	1,188,903	3	4	--	--
Minnesota	2,075,708	17	15	2	--
Northern, Mississippi	671,092	2	2	--	--
Southern, Mississippi	1,126,022	1	2	--	--
Eastern, Missouri	1,621,023	70	31	1	1
Western, Missouri	1,672,302	4	11	1	1
Montana	376,053	12	11	--	--
Nebraska	1,192,214	29	11	--	--
Nevada	81,875	2	5	--	--
New Hampshire	430,572	2	3	--	--
New Jersey	2,537,167	9	14	--	--
New Mexico	327,301	10	12	--	--
Northern, New York	1,862,630	12	16	3	--
Eastern, New York	2,184,429	8	4	1	--
Southern, New York	3,510,226	29	25	1	--
Western, New York	1,556,329	5	8	--	--
Eastern, North Carolina	1,119,593	2	1	--	--
Western, North Carolina	1,086,649	11	19	--	--
North Dakota	577,056	86	17	--	--
Northern, Ohio	2,405,181	9	32	--	--
Southern, Ohio	2,361,940	9	6	--	--
Eastern, Oklahoma	834,395	29	15	--	--

District Court	Population	Commenced during the fiscal year ended 30 June:			
		1918	1919	1920	1921
Western, Oklahoma	822,760	2	7	--	--
Oregon	672,765	11	23	--	--
Eastern, Pennsylvania	2,826,891	9	6	--	--
Middle, Pennsylvania	1,874,310	9	27	--	--
Western, Pennsylvania	2,963,910	11	8	--	--
Puerto Rico	1,118,012	8	6	--	--
Rhode Island	542,610	6	4	--	--
Eastern, South Carolina	857,517	8	5	--	--
Western, South Carolina	657,883	9	7	1	--
South Dakota	583,888	25	2	1	--
Eastern, Tennessee	723,232	4	8	--	--
Middle, Tennessee	804,251	3	14	--	--
Western, Tennessee	657,306	--	2	--	--
Northern, Texas	1,160,676	11	14	--	--
Eastern, Texas	1,004,663	3	5	--	--
Southern, Texas	660,860	64	18	--	--
Western, Texas	1,070,343	46	38	5	--
Utah	373,351	2	9	--	--
Vermont	355,956	2	--	--	--
Eastern, Virginia	1,029,806	--	4	--	--
Western, Virginia	1,031,806	4	3	--	--
Eastern, Washington	409,699	3	14	--	--
Western, Washington	732,291	22	24	8	--

		Commenced during the fiscal year ended 30 June:			
District Court	Population	1918	1919	1920	1921
Northern, W. Virginia	614,224	18	16	1	--
Southern, W. Virginia	606,895	4	6	--	--
Eastern, Wisconsin	1,243,932	7	24	--	--
Western, Wisconsin	1,089,928	18	43	--	--
Wyoming	145,965	2	--	--	--

		1918	1919	1920	1921	Subtotals
SUBTOTAL	87 districts	988	968	40	6	2,002
	Terminated	492	1,179	202	41	1,914
	Convictions	363	514	47	9	933
	Acquittals	57	109	12	3	181
	Nol. pros. or discontinued	51	462	129	23	665
	Quashed or dismissed, demurrer, etc.	21	94	14	6	135

To these totals must be added 133 indictments in the Northern District, Illinois; of these, 96 were convictions. Add also 33 indictments in the District of Kansas (1919); of these, 26 were convictions. Hence, the total number of prosecutions is 2,168, and the total number of convictions is 1,055.[4]

---

[4] See *Report of the Attorney General, 1918*, 179; Peterson and Fite, *Opponents of War*, 240, 245–246.

Total Prosecutions	2,168
Total Convictions	1,055
Total Terminated Before June 30, 1921	2,036

Bibliographical Note

In addition to the manuscript and printed sources cited in the footnotes, the following works were of particular value: Woodrow Wilson, *Leaders of Men,* ed. T. H. Vail Motter (Princeton, 1952), and *Constitutional Government in the United States* (New York, 1908), for Wilson's ideas on leadership. Robert Cushman's instructive studies include "The Impact of War on the Constitution," in *The Impact of War on America* (Ithaca, 1942), and "The Repercussions of Foreign Affairs on the American Tradition of Civil Liberty," *Proceedings of the American Philosophical Society,* XCII (1948). Charles Seymour, "Woodrow Wilson: A Political Balance Sheet," *ibid.,* CI (1957); Edward S. Corwin, "Woodrow Wilson and the Presidency," *Virginia Law Review,* XLII (1956); and the essays in Earl Latham, ed., *The Philosophy and Policies of Woodrow Wilson* (Chicago, 1958), are suggestive analyses although they do not bear directly upon the issue of civil liberties. The invaluable works of the late Zechariah Chafee include *Thirty-five Years with Freedom of Speech* (New York, 1952) and "The Conscription of Public Opinion," in *The Next War: Three Addresses* (Cambridge, 1925).

On the progressive tradition and intervention, see Eric F. Goldman, *Rendezvous with Destiny* (rev. ed., New York, 1956), and Phil L. Snyder, "Carl L. Becker and the Great War: A Crisis for a Humane Intelligence," *Western Political Quarterly,* IX (1956); on war government, Clinton Rossiter, *Constitutional Dictatorship* (Princeton, 1948), and F. L. Paxson, "The American War Government, 1917–1918," *American Historical Review,* XXVI (1920); on the role of the {66} churches, Ray H. Abrams, *Preachers Present Arms* (Philadelphia, 1939); and on military policy, Walter Millis, *Arms and Men* (New York, 1956). Dexter Perkins, *The American Way* (Ithaca, 1957), and John H. Schaar, *Loyalty in America* (Berkeley, 1957), discuss the limits of political deviation.

For a debate on the policies of Gregory and Palmer, see Donald Johnson, "The Political Career of A. Mitchell Palmer," *Pennsylvania History,* XXV (1958); and Harry N. Scheiber, "A. Mitchell Palmer: A Comment," *ibid.,* XXVI (1959).

Works which cast additional light on the subjects suggested by their titles are Lawrence H. Chamberlain, *Loyalty and Legislative Action: A Survey of Activity by the New York State Legislature* (Ithaca, 1951); Herbert A. Miller, "Attitudes toward the Alien in Past Crises," in *Alienage in a Period of Crises* (New York, 1941); Jane Perry Clark, *The Deportation of Aliens from the United States to Europe* (New York, 1931); and, on a subject closely related to the one treated in this essay, *Americanization as a War Measure* (U.S. Department of Interior, Bureau of Education Bulletin, 1918, No. 18 [Washington, 1918]), and Edward G. Hartmann, *The Movement to Americanize the Immigrant* (New York, 1948). Valuable also are the National Civil Liberties Bureau pamphlets in the collection in the Cornell University Library.

Index

Page numbers below reference the pagination of the original 1960 print edition. Those numbers are inserted into the present text by the use of {brackets}. The present edition embeds the original pagination for the convenience of the reader and for continuity in citation, referencing, and classroom assignment across formats and editions.

Alien Act (Oct. 16, 1918), 26–27

Alien enemies: proclamation regarding, 14; internment of, 44–45

Aliens, *see* Foreign-born

Allen, Frederick Lewis, quoted, 52

American Civil Liberties Union, *see* National Civil Liberties Bureau

American Protective League, 43, 47, 49

Americanism and 1916 campaign, 8ff; *see also* Nationalism

Becker, Carl, describes Wilson, 58

Berger, Victor, 38

Bettman, Alfred, 42

Blum, John Morton: on hyphenism, 7; on Burleson, 29; on Wilson, 39

Board of Censorship, 21

Burleson, Albert Sidney, 57; given censorship power, 19–20, 24–25; controls Board of Censorship, 21; administration of censorship, 29ff; and postwar censorship, 34–35, 39; relationship with Wilson, 36ff

Cable and telegraph lines, censorship of, 17

Cahan, Abraham, 34

Censorship, 11, 15–17; demanded by Wilson, 18; under terms of Espionage Act, 19; under terms of Trading-with-Enemy Act, 20–21; under terms of Sedition Act, 24–25; Burleson's

81

administration of, 29ff; in postwar period, 34ff; *see also* Will H. Hays

Chafee, Zechariah, on Burleson, 29

Civil liberties: legislation affecting, 11ff; and postal censorship, 29ff; and Justice Department, 42ff; during Red Scare, 55ff; and Wilson Administration, 59–60; *see also* Censorship, Justice Department, *and* Woodrow Wilson

Civil Service Commission, 14–15

Civil War, security measures during, 12–13

Committee on Public Information, 15–17

Congressional action affecting civil liberties, 12–13, 15, 17–28

Councils of National Defense, 50

Creel, George: and Committee on Public Information, 15; works concerning, cited, 16n; on 1918 election, 40

Croly, Herbert, 38

Culberson, Charles A., 18

Currie, Gilbert A., 23

Cushman, Robert, on civil liberties, 58

Daniels, Josephus, on Lansing, 16

Darrow, Clarence, 58n

Debs, Eugene Victor, 19, 44, 53n

Democratic party: and campaign of 1916, 8; and campaign of 1918, 40

Disloyalty, 5–10; in civil service, 14–15; and pressure for Sedition Act, 22–24; Burleson's definition of, 33–35; warned against by Gregory, 44; condemned by Wilson, 56; *see also* Foreign-born *and* Wilson

Election of 1916, 8–10

Election of 1918, 40

Eliot, Charles W., and preparedness, 4n

Espionage Act, 13, 17ff, 39; tabulation of prosecutions under, 46; sentences commuted, 47; amnesties refused, 57; injustices done under, 57n, 58n; *see also* Sedition Act

Federal employees, 14–15

Foreign-born: praised, 4; condemned for disloyalty, 5, 7ff, 17, 22; identified with radicals, 7

Foreign-language newspapers, 34n; censorship of, 33ff

Freedom of speech and press, see Censorship and Civil liberties

Freeman's Journal, barred from mails, 32

Gardner, Augustus, 2

Garraty, John A., quoted, 57

German-Americans, 4, 7, 50; *see also* Foreign-born

German-language press, 20–21, 33ff

Germany and the United States, 7, 22-23

Gompers, Samuel, 32, 58n

Gregory, Thomas W., 38; and Sedition Act, 23–26; personal views on civil liberties, 28, 42; administration of security legislation, 42ff; relationship with Wilson, 49ff

Hapgood, Norman, 58n

Hays, Will H., and *Liberator* case, 34–35

Haywood, Bill, 48

Hilton, O. A., quoted, 39

Holmes, Oliver Wendell: on judiciary, 43; on wartime offenders, 58n

Hughes, Charles Evans, and 1916 election, 9–10

Immigration legislation, 26–27

Industrial Workers of the World, 21, 44, 48, 50, 59

Irish-Americans, 4, 7; *see also* Foreign-born

Justice Department: introduces security legislation, 11; administration of security legislation, 42ff; and American Protective League, 43, 49; district attorneys' freedom of action, 44ff; administration centralized, 46, 51; *see also* Thomas W. Gregory

Labor unions identified with radicalism, 54

La Follette, Robert, 4

La Follette Seamen's Act, 7

Lansing, Robert, 16, 16n

Leader, barred from mails, 31, 37

League of Nations tour, Woodrow Wilson's, 55–56

Liberator censorship case, 34–35

Lincoln, Abraham, 12–13

Link, Arthur S., 31n; on 1916 election, 10

Loyalty, *see* Disloyalty *and* Wilson

Lusitania incident, 3–4

Lynching, 50–51

Masses, barred from mails, 31, 36

Mob violence: Negro lynchings, 50n; Prager lynching, 51

Morgan, J. P., and Co., 3

Nation: barred from mails, 32; on Burleson, 36

National Civil Liberties Bureau, 20n, 33, 33n, 48

Nationalism, 40, 59

Nativism, 7, 59

Navy Department, 17

Negroes, 43n, 50n, 54n

Neutrality, 1–3

O'Brian, John Lord, 42, 57n; on propaganda, 17; on postal officials, 29

O'Hare, Kate Richards, 47

O'Leary, Jeremiah, 9

Overman, Lee S., 12

Pacifists, 4, 7

Palmer, A. Mitchell, 54, 57, 66

Pinchot, Amos, 3, 36

Postal censorship, *see* Censorship

Postal Classification Act of 1879, 31

Praeger, Otto, 21

Prager, Robert, lynching of, 51

Preparedness movement, 2–3; opposition to, 3–5

Progressives: opposition to preparedness, 3–4; advocate restriction of mailing privileges, 25n; support lost to Wilson, 41

Propaganda, 11–12; in preparedness campaign, 4n; and Committee on Public Information, 16–17; and Sedition Act provisions regarding "dangerous utterances," 22ff

Radicalism: identified with foreign-born, 7; and Burleson, 34; fear of, 54ff

Radicals, opposition to preparedness, 4, 7

Red Scare (1919–20), 27, 52ff

Roosevelt, Franklin D., on preparedness campaign, 4n

Roosevelt, Theodore, 2, 10, 22, 30

Root, Elihu, 57n

Sabotage, 12, 19, 44

Sabotage Act, 22

Sayre, Nevin, 37

Security measures in World War I, 10ff; characterized, 28

Sedition: peacetime sedition act requested, 53; state laws against, 54; *see also* Sedition Act

Sedition Act, 13, 15, 22ff; bill to terminate, 39; *see also* Espionage Act

Sinclair, Upton, 30, 38, 58n

"Slacker raids," 47–48

Socialist newspapers, 32

Socialists, 21, 59; opposition to preparedness, 4, 7

Straight, Willard, 2, 7

Subsidiary press: defined, 20n; censorship of, 33ff

Supreme Court and censorship, 32; *see also* Oliver Wendell Holmes

Swisher, Carl Brent, on Burleson, 29

Threats-against-the-President Act, 13

Trading-with-the-Enemy Act, 20–21

Tumulty, Joe, 6

Villard, Oswald Garrison, 3, 32, 37

Warren, Charles, 49

Webb, Edwin Y., 12, 18, 22

Wilson, Woodrow: neutrality policies of, 1–2; and preparedness movement, 3–4; on foreign-born and disloyalty, 4ff, 17–18, 22–23, 55ff; intolerance of preparedness opponents, 5; rearmament program, 5ff; emphasizes Americanism in 1916 campaign, 8–10; policies compared with Lincoln's, 12–13; on espionage, 17; and censorship, 18, 21, 30–31, 36ff;

approves Sedition Act, 25–26; and immigration legislation, 26; advocates peacetime sedition act, 39, 54; loses liberal support, 40–41, 57–58; relationship with Gregory, 49ff; and mob violence, 51; and Red Scare, 52ff; League tour of, 55ff; last months in office, 56–57; described by Becker, 58; and civil liberties, 59–60

Wise, Stephen S., on preparedness movement, 4n

World (New York), quoted, 32-33

World Tomorrow, barred from mails, 37

About the Author

Harry N. Scheiber is the Stefan A. Riesenfeld Professor of Law (Emeritus) at the University of California at Berkeley. He is also Professor Emeritus of History, Chancellor's Professor Emeritus, Co-Director of the Law of the Sea Institute, and Director of the Institute for Legal Research. He earned his A.B. from Columbia University, his M.A. and Ph.D. degrees from Cornell University, and an Honorary Doctorate in Jurisprudence from Uppsala University in Sweden.

Scheiber did postdoctoral work in law while a fellow at the Center for Advanced Study in the Behavioral Sciences. He taught at Dartmouth from 1960 through 1971, and then became a professor of American history at UC San Diego. He joined the law faculty of UC Berkeley in 1980. He served for eight years as chair and associate dean for the Jurisprudence and Social Policy Program. He has also served as director of Berkeley's Center for the Study of Law and Society.

He has held Guggenheim, Rockefeller, American Council of Learned Societies, National Endowment for the Humanities, and Social Science Research Council Fellowships. He was a Distinguished Fulbright Lecturer in Australia, and he has been president of the Agricultural History Society, the Council for Research in Economic History, and the ACLU of New Hampshire. He was elected in 1999 as an honorary fellow of the American Society for Legal History. In 2003, he was elected as fellow of the American Academy of Arts and Sciences.

Scheiber has written extensively in American legal history, especially on the history of law and public policy, on federalism, and on constitutional development. He has also led research projects and written on aspects of environmental law, especially Law of the Sea and ocean resources policy. His books include *Law of the Sea: The Common Heritage and Emerging Challenges*; *Legal Cultures and the Legal Profession*; *Inter-Allied Conflict and Modern Ocean Law Origins, 1945-52*; *American Law and the Constitutional Order*; *American Economic History*; *Ohio Canal Era—A Case Study of Government and the Economy*; *The Old Northwest—Studies in Regional History*; *Perspectives on Federalism*; *Federalism and the Judicial Mind*; *The State and Freedom of Contract*; *Earl Warren and the Warren Court*; *Bringing New Law to Ocean Waters*; and *The Oceans in the Nuclear Age*.

Visit us at *www.quidprobooks.com*.

www.ingramcontent.com/pod-product-compliance
Lightning Source LLC
Chambersburg PA
CBHW070934160426
43193CB00011B/1684